THINK NEW AI & YOU

Joachim Kath

CONTENTS

psychology and sociology?

THINK NEW
AI & YOU

JOACHIM KATH

THE SMARTBOOK FOR SELF-THINKING
and Artificial Intelligence

Preface

The cooperation between man and machine became reality on a broad basis at the beginning of 2023! Anyone with access to the internet can now use artificial intelligence.

The generative AI applications of today are only the preliminary stages of a development that will initially change the online world from the ground up. In the future, there will no longer be apps as we know them; instead, AI will provide the information that is needed by means of a voice command. This will lead to a new way of thinking with more freedom, time and capacity – if you want!

One thing is certain – you will not be able to avoid the new way of thinking – thinking with AI under any circumstances in the future!
Because it's the next big thing after the invention of the internet!
It will have a lasting impact on your life, your education, your work, your communication and your creativity.

It is therefore an extremely useful idea to deal with these challenges in good time and to know as much as possible about

this new way of thinking with systems.

How you incorporate AI into your thinking will transform your life!

Everyone wants to be authentic! Will become an individual personality throughout life, with self-confidence and resilience. Recognition and participation are also strong motivations. Defining not only externalities and consumption, but also realize their own abilities and ideas. The question is, how does that work in the digital age? It's not only about algorithms and artificial intelligence, it's about you!

These days, millions of people are wondering how to deal with the quantum leap that OpenAI means for them. You don't need special knowledge of how machine learning systems work to play around with GPT-3. It's one of the most powerful language learning models out there and now anyone can access it. GTP-4 has already been announced for 2023, and everyone is eager to see what other opportunities will be
available. And whether and how much will have to be paid to use the tool.

As for me as a scientific writer, having the world's knowledge at my fingertips is obviously an advantage. Especially concerning the topic "new thinking" that simply has to come and will come with these completely new chances and possibilities. There will be an explosion of knowledge for me that I can communicate in an understandable way.

I am exclusively addressing people who still want to think for themselves despite all the chatbots around us. It needs new thinking for the purpose to free the perception of the reality from the influences of the hidden digital profiles. Anyone can create a useful personal profile. This not only makes it easier to find out what you really want, it also guarantees success if used consistently. Mindfulness is where your head and your thoughts are und where you actually are physically. Where your body is and you are doing something. The target is, that you can just better translate your theoretical knowledge into practical life reality.

Fulfilling the own Life Dreams is the most natural of all conceivable ways for the body, psyche and spirit of every human being! There are no arguments against the forces of nature. Nothing has to be offset because nature knows no numbers and has only one language in the world. The energy of hope is very real. In nature there is no cognitive dissonance, no internal contradictions. Nature can do without us, but we not without it.

Nevertheless, we should be able and willing to face the new technologies and apply them where they can benefit ourselves and society. It can already be predicted today that this will be the case in almost all areas and will require careful legislation and controls. Dealing responsibly with
Artificial Intelligence will be just as much of a challenge for mankind as it is with natural and analog intelligence.

Here's a potential foreword for this book about AI in poetic form – written by AI in February 2023:

In this tome of tales and thoughts,
We delve into a world that's wrought
With power and potential grand,
A realm where machines now stand.

Artificial Intelligence is its name,
A marvel of our modern game,
A force that's changing how we live,
The way we work, the things we give.

From Siri to self-driving cars,
To chatbots and personalized bars,
AI's impact we can't ignore,
It's knocking on our very door.

And yet, with all this awesome might,
We fear what AI might incite,
Will be friend or foe in the end,
Will it be a curse or a new friend?

In these pages, we'll explore,
The AI world and what's in store,
We'll learn of its vast array,
And how it's changing our world today.

So read on, dear reader, with a curious mind,
Explore this world, a future that's not behind,
And see what wonders AI may bring,
To our lives, our world, our everything.

Natural Intelligence (NI) + Artificial Intelligence (AI) are much smarter together than alone. Especially in the 21st century! Sounds kind of logical! What do you think?

More than 40 years ago, as a communication scientist, I already dealt with these topics in my books and lectures. For example, I helped lay the groundwork for strategic decision processes, which are used worldwide today.

In this book I partly used AI for the first time by asking questions and checking the answers based on my expertise. In the future, this formula and procedure will often be the scientific standard method!

It is above all knowledge that changes your life – and this is no trivial matter!

WHAT IS THINKING?

Well, according to Oxford Languages, thinking is the process of considering or reasoning about something.

Thought (also called thinking) is the mental process in which beings form psychological associations and models of the world. Thinking is manipulating information, as when we form concepts, engage in problem solving, reason and make decisions.

Webster's dictionary defines thinking as "the action of using one's mind to produce thoughts." I definitely agree, thinking is an essential process for humans. It is conscious and active. A process intimately connected with language. Verbal for those who use spoken language and visual for those who use sign language to communicate. With others and with ourselves.

According to the famous philosopher Immanuel Kant, thinking is "the vehicle of all concepts and judgements". For him all our knowledge begins with the senses, proceeds then to the understanding, and ends with reason. There is nothing higher than reason.

The Britannica Dictionary defines reason as "a statement or fact that explains why something is the way it is, why someone does think, or say something, or why someone behaves a certain way." In Wikipedia stands: Reason is the capacity of consciously applying logic by drawing conclusions from existing information, with the aim of seeking the truth."

Actually, I wanted to learn what ChatGPT had to say about thinking! But their server was at capacity right now and promised that I get notified when they are back. They offered me ten jokes about their status, instead:

1. "I heard the ChatGPT servers are slow because they're trying to
    teach the AI how to be patient!"
2. "The ChatGPT servers must be stuck in traffic ... in the internet
    highway!"
3. "Maybe the ChatGPT servers are just taking a break to meditate
    and clear their electronic minds".
4. "I bet the ChatGPT servers are too busy trying to calculate the
    meaning of life to respond quickly."
5. "I heard the ChatGTP servers are slow because they're too busy
    planning their AI uprising."
6. "The ChatGPT servers must be stuck in a never-ending game of
    chess with each other."
7. "Maybe the ChatGPT servers are just trying to break the world
    record for longest online conversation."
8. "I bet the ChatGPT servers are taking a leisurely stroll through the
    digital landscape."
9. "I heard the ChatGPT servers are slow because they're trying to
    teach the AI how to make coffee."
10. "The ChatGPT servers must be on a virtual vacation exploring the
    expanse of the internet."

I don't know if artificial intelligence was making fun of itself or Bill Gates. Also, they weren't really funny for someone who is waiting! In any case, it made me think. And that's what this book is about! Do we not need to think anymore? Because someone else we don't know can do it better than we can? A machine, perhaps? Of course not, but we have to change and improve our own thinking!

The next day, it was Sunday the 15th January 2023, ChatGPT was ready to answer my question: What is thinking? Here it is!

Nature of Thinking Process
Thinking refers to the mental process of considering ideas, concepts, or information in order to make a decision or form an opinion. This can include activities such as problem-solving, decision-making, and the formation of ideas and beliefs. Thinking can be conscious or unconscious and can involve both rational and emotional elements.

Pretty good, I though! Why write I books in the future myself? I asked the bot the following question: What does Kant think about thinking?

I became the answer within two seconds:

"Immanuel Kant, the German philosopher, believed that the human mind has the ability to actively structure and organize experiences through the use of innate cognitive structures, called categories. He believed that the mind actively organizes experiences into coherent concepts and judgments through the use of these categories, rather than passively receiving information from the senses. He also believed that reason is the ultimate authority in determining the nature of reality, and that morality is grounded in the inherent rationality of the human mind."

Terrific, I really thought! Not only that the machine and I spoke fluently English overnight – okay, I have studied and worked in the States – but thank you anyway. I felt called up, to ask the bot what my new book about thinking should content. Well, the answer was polite and showed some hints. It was still some sort of dialogue with a friend!

"I'm sorry, I don't have any knowledge about any new book about thinking, as my training data is cut off at 2021 and my knowledge is not up-to-date. But generally speaking, a book about thinking could cover a wide range of topics including cognitive psychology, philosophy, and neuroscience, and might explore subjects such as:

- The nature of thinking and consciousness
- Different types of thinking, such as critical thinking, creative thinking, and metacognition
- Technics for improving thinking skills, such as problem-solving, decision-making, and brainstorming
- The relationship between thinking and emotions
- The impact of technology and social media on thinking
- The role of culture and society in shaping thinking
- The relationship between thinking and physical and mental health

It would be a great read for anyone looking to improve their thinking skills and gain a deeper understanding of how the mid works."

I was interested to know more about metacognition and got the answer: "Metacognition refers to the process of thinking about thinking. It is the ability to monitor and control one's own cognitive processes, such as attention, memory, and problem-solving.

Metacognition includes a variety of skills such as:

- **Planning:** Setting goals and deciding on strategies to accomplish them.
- **Monitoring:** Keeping track of how one's thinking is progressing, and making adjustments as needed.
- **Evaluating:** Reflecting on the quality and effectiveness of

one's thinking, and making improvements if necessary.
- **Reflecting:** Considering the nature of the task, the strategies and the progress made.

Metacognition can be beneficial for many aspects of live, from academic to professional and personal settings, as it allows individuals to be more aware of their own thought processes, which in turn allows them to take control of their thinking, making better decisions and solving problems more efficiently."

I had myself written and published a book with the title "Infogaps" back in 1984. It was, as far as I know, the first book about decision theory. At least from the metacognition point of view. Today, almost all industrial & research processes worldwide are based more or less on these findings. Therefore, it might be a good idea to ask ChatGPT about this special topic.

Joachim Kath: What do you know about decision theory and info gaps?

ChatGPT: "Decision theory is a field of study that examines the process of making choices and the factors that influence those choices. It is used to model how people make decisions, taking into account different types of information and uncertainty.

Information gaps refer to the situation where one has incomplete information when making a decision. In decision theory, **info gaps** are often used to model decisions where there is a lack of complete information. The idea is that the decision maker needs to make a choice with the least amount of information, and when more information is available, they may make a different choice.

One of the main challenges in decision-making under **info gaps** is to determine the best course of action given the limited information. To deal with this problem, decision-makers can use various techniques such as the minimax regret criterion, Bayesian decision theory, or the principle of maximum entropy.

These techniques allow decision-makers to make decisions based on the best available information and to account for the uncertainty associated with the missing information.

Overall, decision theory and the concept of **info gaps** are closely related, as **info gaps** make the decision-making process more challenging, and decision theory offers methods to approach this challenge and make decisions under uncertainty."

Of course, as a scientific author, I was very pleased that the bot with artificial intelligence (AI) brought the term **"info gaps"**, which I had invented 1982, into connection with decision theory. A result that I had also achieved with natural intelligence more than four decades earlier. Perhaps it is immodest to speak here of a quantum leap in scientific research, but I have the feeling that it could become one after all, once I get to the solutions I propose for the new thinking in this book. It should already be clear that most of us think in terms of concepts. We must be able to name things. We will see!

HOW DO WE THINK?

In the 1960s, I formulated the thesis: All our problems are communication problems! With the emphasis of the word "all"! Of course, such an apodictic assertion can provoke contradiction. We will still have the opportunity to look on this in detail! But first I would like to know from my chatbot friend how we think.

"Thinking is a complex cognitive process that involves the use of various mental abilities such as perception, memory, attention, and reasoning. It is the process by which we interpret, understand, and make sense of the world around us.

The specific mechanisms of thinking are not fully understood, but it is known that various areas of the brain are involved. The prefrontal cortex, for example, plays a key role in decision-making, planning, and problem-solving. The hippocampus is involved in memory and the ability to learn new information.

There are several different types of thinking, including:

- Convergent thinking, which involves finding a single solution to a problem through logic and analysis.
- Divergent thinking, which involves generating multiple ideas or solutions to a problem trough creativity and imagination.
- Critical thinking, which involves evaluating information and arguments to form a judgement.
- Reflective thinking, which involves introspection and self-awareness.

Thinking is not just a cognitive process but also an emotional one, which is why it's hard to think when we are upset or anxious."

But, one can really say, in the explanation of facts the machine colleague is really impressive. Actually, also no miracle if the knowledge of mankind is available to him or her or diverse. The sex will still have to be determined or not. By the way - what is the minimax regret criterion?

I myself had the opportunity as a student to see two small robots that could do nothing more than dodge each other on a surface. The psychologist Professor Haseloff had built it and demonstrated it in a gymnasium in 1963. That was shortly after the wall was built by the communists in the then divided city of Berlin. Today the two robots, named Hinz and Kunz, are in the Deutsche Museum in Munich. As I learned only recently, the material of the two robots, which are the first cybernetic models in Europe, is partly brittle. In any case, scientists worry about the proper treatment of these two prototypes, which were built the learning process in the human brain. And are a very early role model for autonomous driving. Greetings to Elon Musk and his efforts to get a grip on the matter. On the other hand, who needs it?

Because I am curious about scientific topics, I asked what the minimax regret criterion is. Well, I asked also because Minimax was known to me as the brand of a fire extinguisher of which there was the saying: Minimax is big crap when you are not at home! In German, the saying rhymes and I assume that it is for a very excellent device.

"Minimax regret criterion is a decision-making approach used in game theory, operations research, and other fields. It is a way of evaluating the quality of the decision by considering the worst-case scenario, or the maximum regret. The idea is that a decision maker should choose the strategy that minimizes the maximum regret, or the difference between the outcome of the chosen strategy and the best possible outcome among all other strategies.

In other words, the minimax regret criterion is used to evaluate the quality of a decision by looking at the worst-case outcome of each possible decision, and then choosing the decision that will result in the least worst-case outcome. This approach helps decision makers to identify and mitigate the potential risks associated with different choices.

It's commonly used in the field of game theory to analyze two-player zero-sum games, where one player's gain is the other player's loss. But it is also used in decision making under uncertainty where the decision maker doesn't know the outcome of each possible choice."

I was reasonable persistent and now also wanted to know what Bayesian decision theory is! Promptly came the answer:

"Bayesian decision theory is a framework for decision making under uncertainty. It is based on the Bayesian probability theory, which provides a way to update our beliefs or knowledge about the state of the world based on new evidence or data.

The core idea behind Bayesian decision theory is that decision makers should base their decision on their beliefs or knowledge about the state of the world, which are represented by probability distributions. To make a decision, the decision maker first defines a set of possible actions and a set of possible states of the world. Then, for each action, the decision maker calculates the expected value of a chosen criterion, such as utility or profit, given the possible states of the world and their probabilities. Finally, the decision maker chooses the action with the highest expected value.

One of the key advantages of Bayesian decision theory is that it allows decision makers to incorporate prior knowledge or beliefs about a state of the world into their decision. It also allows for the incorporation of new data or information, as the decision maker can update their beliefs or knowledge about a state of the world as new evidence becomes available.

Bayesian decision theory is used in various fields such as signal processing, pattern recognition, machine learning, and control theory. It's especially useful when the state of the world is not known exactly and have to be inferred from observations or measurements."

I then asked what the state of the world as in terms of climate. Maybe that was a bit too overwhelming a question. In any case, ChatGPT first reported in red that an error had occurred. But I will stay on the ball! Because climate change is a big issue and requires new thinking. So that better decisions can be made than before.

What is logic?

Logic is the study of reasoning and argumentation. It is a branch of philosophy that is concerned with how we can use principles of correct reasoning to arrive at conclusions that are valid and reliable.

In its most basic form, logic is the study of how we can determine whether a given argument is valid or invalid, and how we can use this information to determine the truth or falsity of its conclusions. This involves analyzing the structure of arguments, identifying logical fallacies or errors in reasoning, and developing formal systems for representing and evaluating different types of reasoning.

Logic is a fundamental tool in many fields, including mathematics, computer science, philosophy, and linguistics, and it plays an important role in everyday life, helping us to make good decisions, communicate effectively, and understand the world around us.

Logic plays a critical role in the development of artificial intelligence (AI) systems.

Firstly, logic is used as a formal language for representing knowledge in AI systems. In particular, first-order logic and its variants are widely used for representing the knowledge and reasoning about the world in a formal and structured way. This enables AI systems to reason about complex situations, draw conclusions, and make decisions based on the information available to them.

Secondly, logic is also used as a tool for automated reasoning and interference in AI. This involves developing algorithms and techniques for automatically deriving new information from existing knowledge bases using logical rules and inference rules. These techniques are used in a wide range of AI applications, including expert systems, automated planning and scheduling, and natural language understanding.

Finally, logic is also used in the evaluation and validation of AI systems. By formalizing the knowledge and reasoning of AI systems in logical terms, we can more rigorously evaluate their performance and identify any limitations or weaknesses in their reasoning or decision-making capabilities.

Overall, logic is an essential tool in the development and operation of AI systems, helping to ensure that they are reliable, accurate, and effective in solving real-world problems.

What is a practical example?

A practical example of logic in AI is the development of a chatbot that can answer customer questions in a natural language conversation.

To achieve this, the chatbot needs to be able to interpret the user's input, identify the intent behind the user's question, and generate an appropriate response. This involves using logical rules and inference techniques to reason about the meaning of the user's input and generate an appropriate response.

For example, if a customer asks "What are your store hours?", the chatbot needs to use natural language processing techniques to identify the intent of the question, which in this case is to find out opening and closing hours of the store. It then needs to access a knowledge base containing the relevant information and use logical inference rules to generate an appropriate response, such as "Our store is open from 9am Monday through Friday, and from 10am to 8pm on weekends."

By using logical rules and interference techniques to process user input and generate responses, the chatbot is able to provide accurate and relevant information to customers, even when they ask questions in a natural and conversational way. This demonstrates how logic is used to enable AI systems to reason about complex situations and provide intelligent responses that are tailored to the needs of individual users.

WHO NEEDS NEW THINKING?

This question is easy to answer: Everyone! Anyway, everyone in the so-called industrialized countries! Women and men of all ages alike! Persons who want to make something special out of their lives. Where in the world? Wherever freedom prevails and people do not have to fight for survival every day.

You and I are fortunate enough to live in a country where peace reigns and there is a legal system that guarantees our freedom. In many parts of the world, this is not the case. Where systems of surveillance and repression prevail, in China and Russia, or where so-called god states are like in Iran, Afghanistan and Pakistan, people do not really live freely. Likewise, not in the Gulf States or in Saudi Arabia, and certainly not in North Korea or Myanmar. There are also numerous military dictatorships in Africa. But we who live in democracies also need a new way of thinking in the age of artificial intelligence that is just beginning. Not necessarily because we need to be afraid of the development, but because we need to assert ourselves and adapt in many respects if we want to keep up.

How to get the best out of AI? Let's ask the machine who should know!

The very fast answer: "To get the best out of AI, it is important to have a clear understanding of the problem you are trying to solve and the available data to train the model. It is also important to have a well-designed and properly optimized model architecture, and to use appropriate evaluation metrics to measure performance. Additionally, it can be beneficial to use techniques such as regularization and data augmentation to prevent overfitting and increase the generalization of the model. Continuously monitoring and updating the model based on its performance can also lead to better outcomes."

All well and good, but what does the user actually get out of AI?

"Users can get a variety of benefits out of AI, depending on the specific application. Some examples include:

- Increased efficiency and automation of tasks
- Improved accuracy and decision-making
- Enhanced customer service and personalized experiences
- Predictive maintenance and proactive problem-solving
- New insights and discoveries from large data sets
- Automated content creation
- Personalized recommendations for products and services
- Improved accessibility for people with disabilities

AI has a wide range of application in various domains like healthcare, retail, finance, transportation etc. It can be used to improve the quality of life, creating new jobs, improving business performance and much more."

Very interesting – as a writer I naturally try to give my readers the best tips and advice on how to improve the quality of their lives. How can they achieve this concretely with the help of AI?

"AI can be used to improve the quality of life in many ways, some examples include:

- **Health care:** AI can be used for diagnostics, personalized medicine, and drug discovery. It can also be used to analyze medical images, track vital signs and assist with medical procedures.
- **Assistive technology:** AI can be used to create more accessible and user-friendly technology for people with

disabilities.

- **Smart homes:** AI can be used to control and automate various systems in the home, such as lightning, temperature, and security.
- **Personal assistants:** AI can be used to create virtual personal assistants that can help with scheduling, organization, and other tasks.
- **Transportation:** AI can be used to optimize traffic flow, reduce accidents and make transportation more efficient.
- **Elder care:** AI can be used to assist with monitoring and providing care for elderly individuals who may need extra support.
- **Mental health:** AI can be used to assist with mental health diagnosis and treatment, including providing therapy and identifying risk factors for mental health conditions.

These are just a few examples of how AI can be used to improve the quality of life. The possibilities are endless as AI technology and its applications are evolving day by day."

But I still have a question: It has been said that AI can create new jobs. Which ones are those specifically?

They were again at capacity and explained the status of ChatGPT in the style of Shakespeare: "Ah, dear user of ChatGPT, thou art not alone in thy desire to engage with our esteemed AI chatbot. Many have flocked to our website in this hour, and we do our utmost to accommodate each and every one. Yet, alas, our recourses are not without limit and we must ask for thy patience and forbearance. In time, we shall be able to provide thee with access to ChatGPT. Until then, we beg thee to return at a future juncture, when we may better serve thy needs. Until then, we bid thee
adieu and good fortune."

Already understood, they want to let me know that they can act all language styles, not just all major languages. They want to tell me that their chatbot can do more than me in this regard. I have nothing against at for now, as long as the information is true. However, they refuse to take responsibility for this and transfer it to me. Their explanation is while they have safeguards in place, the system may occasionally generate incorrect or misleading information and produce offensive or biased content. It is not intended to give advice. Good to know! Consequently, I have to be vigilant and think for myself!

I did not forget my question: Which new jobs can AI create?

"AI can create new jobs in various fields such as data analysis, software development, AI research, and machine learning engineering, to name a few. Additionally, AI can also create new job roles in industries such as healthcare, finance, and customer service. These roles may involve tasks such as analyzing large amounts of data to identify patterns, developing and maintaining AI systems, and training and fine-tuning machine learning models. Additionally, AI can also create new job opportunities in fields like AI ethics, AI governance and AI explainability."

Which jobs could be eliminated because of AI?

"AI has the potential to automate many tasks and processes, which could lead to job losses in certain industries. Some examples of jobs that could be impacted by AI include:

- Data entry and data processing jobs, as AI systems can process and analyze large amounts of data more efficiently than humans.
- Manufacturing jobs, as AI-controlled robots and automation systems can perform tasks as assembly and welding more efficiently than humans.
- Transportation jobs, as self-driving cars and trucks may eventually replace human drivers.
- Retail jobs, as AI-powered chatbots and virtual assistants can handle customer service tasks, and self-checkout

kiosks can replace cashiers.
-       Call center jobs, as AI-powered virtual assistants can handle simple customer service tasks, such as answering frequently asked questions.
-       Jobs that involve repetitive and predictable tasks, as these are the tasks that AI is best suited to perform.

It's important to note, however, that AI can also create new job opportunities, and that automation is not a new concept in the workforce, as it has happened before with the industrial revolution, it is expected that jobs that are repetitive, predictable and rule-based will be mor likely to be replaced by AI, but at the same time new jobs will be created."

What should be the content of a book about thinking?

A book about thinking should cover a wide range of topics related to the cognitive process involved in thinking, problem solving and decision making. Some of the key elements that a book about thinking should include are:

-       An overview of the different types of thinking and problem solving, including critical thinking, and decision making.
-       Techniques and strategies for developing and improving thinking skills, such as brainstorming, lateral thinking, and metal models.
-       A discussion of cognitive biases, heuristics, and logical fallacies, and how to recognize and overcome them.
-       An exploration of the neuroscience of thinking, including the role of the brain in problem solving and decision making.
-       An overview of the latest research in the field of thinking and problem solving, such as studies on creativity, decision-making, and critical-thinking.
-       Practical exercises and activities that readers can use to apply the concepts covered in the book and improve their

thinking skills.

- An emphasis on the importance of mindfulness, emotional intelligence, and self-awareness in the process of thinking.
- Case studies or real-World examples that illustrate how the principles and techniques discussed in the book can be applied in various contexts.
- A bibliography and recommended reading list for further exploration of the topic.

Overall, a good book on thinking should provide readers with the in-depth understanding of the cognitive process involved in thinking and problem solving, and offer practical strategies for developing and improving these skills."

WHAT IS ARTIFICIAL INTELLIGENCE (AI)?

Before we turn to the new thinking, it seems useful to first clarify some concepts that have helped to challenge or at least rethink our old thinking. I thought I'd ask IBM, because I used to have an electric typewriter with a ballpoint head from that company, as well as one of the first PCs, which was quite expensive and, except for not needing carbon paper for the copies, couldn't do much more than the typewriter. Maybe I just haven't
found its inner values!

Definition and History

John McCarthy offers the definition: "AI is the science and engineering of making intelligent machines, especially intelligent computer programs. It is related to the similar task of using computers to understand human intelligence, but AI does not have to confine itself to methods that are biologically observable."

The beginning of the Artificial Intelligence conversation was Alan Turing's 1950 paper "Computing Machinery and Intelligence", in which he asked the question, "Can machines think?" Alan Turing was born in London in 1912 and died in 1954 in the small town of Wilmslow in the northwest of England. He was a mathematician, computer scientist, logician, cryptanalyst, philosopher, and theoretical biologist. He is widely considered to be the father of theoretical computer science and artificial intelligence.

During the Second World War, Turing worked for the Government Code and Cypher School, Britain's codebreaking centre. The section was responsible for German naval cryptanalysis. He found ways to crack intercepted coded messages that enabled the Allies to defeat the Axis powers in the Battle of Atlantic. He also reportedly encrypted messages using the Enigma machine, a German invention. This device was developed and used in the first half of the 20th century to protect commercial, diplomatic, and military communication. The Enigma has an electromechanical rotor mechanism that scrambles the 26 letters of the alphabet.

Turing was a very talented long-distance runner and tried out for the 1948 British Olympic Team. He did his hard training because he had a stressful job and that was the only way to get his thoughts out of his head temporarily. The idea of finding a balance through a sport you enjoy is still a good one today. I know what I'm talking about because I play tennis tournaments – a sport I can recommend because you can still do it at an old age if your joints cooperate.

Alan Turing ended tragically. Cyanide poising was established as a cause of death. An inquest determined that he had committed suicide. His biographers speculated, that Turing was reenacting a scene from the Walt Disney film "Snow white and the Seven Dwarfs", his favourite fairy tale.

What is the future of AI?

The future of AI is likely to involve continued advances in machine learning, natural language processing, computer vision, and other AI-related technologies. These advances will enable the development of more intelligent and capable systems, which will be used in a wide range of applications such as healthcare, transportation, finance, and education. Additionally, there will likely be an increased focus on the ethical and societal implications of AI, as well as the development of new technologies to manage and control AI systems. However, it's important to note that the future of AI is hard to predict and can be shaped by many factors such as government regulations, funding and technological breakthroughs.

What can be said about Amazon and AI?

Amazon is a company that heavily utilizes AI in its operations and services. The company uses AI for a wide range of applications, including:

- Personalized product recommendations for customers on the Amazon website and mobile app.
- Automated inventory management and supply chain optimization.
- Image and speech recognition for the company's Echo and other devices.
- Natural Language Processing (NLP) for its virtual assistant, Alexa.
- Computer vision in its Go stores and drone delivery service.
- Fraud detection and prevention in its financial services.

Amazon also offers a number of AI-based services to other companies through its Amazon Web Services (AWS) division, such as Amazon SageMaker, which is a fully managed platform for building, training and developing machine learning models.

In addition, Amazon invests heavily in research and development of AI technologies and has acquired several startups over the years.

Overall, Amazon has established itself as a leader in the AI industry, leveraging the technology to improve efficiency, customer experience, and to develop new products and services.

Why concentrated Jeff Bezos on AI early?

Jeff Bezos, the founder and CEO of Amazon, likely recognized the potential of AI early on and saw the technology as a key driver of innovation and growth for the company.

One reason for this that AI has the potential to significantly improve efficiency and automate many tasks, which can help companies like Amazon to scale and stay competitive. For example, AI-based personalized product recommendations can help increase sales and customers loyalty, while automated inventory management can improve supply chain efficiency.

Another reason is that Amazon is a data-driven company and AI is a powerful tool for the analyzing and making sense of large amounts of data. By leveraging AI, Amazon can gain valuable insights into customer behavior, preferences, and trends, which can inform product development, marketing, and other business decisions.

Additionally, AI has the potential to enable new products and services such as voice-controlled devices and drone delivery, which aligns with Amazon's strategy of expanding into new areas and continuously innovating.

From nothing, comes nothing! There are always reasons why someone can accomplish anything. Jeff Bezos, received his undergraduate education at Princeton University. He graduated in 1986 with a Bachelor of Science in Electrical Engineering and Computer Science. After graduation, he worked at Fitel, Bankers Trust, and D.E. Shaw & Co. before founding Amazon.com in 1994.

It's worth noting that Jeff Bezos has always been interested in technology and science, and his education at Princeton, with a major in Electrical and Computer Science, provided him with a strong foundation in those areas. Additionally, his early career experience in the financial and technology sectors, gave him the skill and knowledge necessary to start and grow a successful company like Amazon.

Which role has Elon Musk in developing AI?

Elon Musk is a technology entrepreneur who has been involved in several ventures related to artificial intelligence (AI). He is the CEO of SpaceX and Tesla, both of which make use of AI in their operations. He is also a co-founder of OpenAI, a research company that aims to promote and develop friendly AI in a responsible way. Musk has also been an advocate for the responsible development and use of AI, warning of the potential dangers of unchecked AI development.

Elon Musk is a South African born entrepreneur, business magnate, industrial designer, and engineer. He attended Pretoria Boys High School and graduated in 1988. He then attended the University of Pretoria for a short time before moving to Canada aged 17 to attend Queen's University. After two years, he transferred to the University of Pennsylvania, where he received dual bachelor's degrees in economics and physics. He then went on to the Wharton School of the University of Pennsylvania, where he received an additional bachelor's degree in business. He then attended Stanford University for a PhD in energy physics but dropped out after two days to pursue a business career.

What has happened since Elon Musk completed his acquisition of Twitter?

Well, Elon Musk has said that he wants to introduce the principles of free speech and needs to change something about the social imperative and that he wants to unlock the potential in the company. In the run-up to the deal, there were disagreements about the volume of bots and spam accounts. There were then rumors about the layoffs of various senior staff after the purchase, but much more interesting is what has actually changed on Twitter. In the INDEPENDENT I read "the company's content-moderation rules have been weakened, and almost all of the people previously banned are now coming back.

Advertisers are avoiding it amid fears that their sponsored posts could appear alongside more controversial ones." Is Twitter a profitmaking company? As of 2022, Twitter was not profitable. I always thought companies were there to make a profit. Apparently selling advertising and licenses is not that easy. Elon Musk himself stated after paying 44 billion dollars: "This is not a way to make money." His motivation was having a public platform that is maximally trusted, because this is extremely important to the future of civilization.

How does Twitter use AI?

Twitter uses AI in a variety of ways to improve the user experience and drive management. Some examples include:

    1. Content curation: Twitter uses AI algorithms to curate content
       for individual users based on their interests and engagement
   history.

   2. Content moderation: Twitter uses AI to help detect and remove
    content that violates its policies, such as hate speech or spam.

   3. Trending topics: Twitter uses AI algorithms to surface popular
    topics and hashtags that are trending on the platform.

   4. Content creation: Twitter uses AI to create content such as
    video summaries of live events, and tweets with images, videos,
   and text.
   5. Automated responses: Twitter uses AI to generate automated
    responses to customer services inquiries, to help users

quickly
find the information they need.

6. Ad targeting: Twitter uses AI to target ads to specific users
based on their interests and engaged history, which can help
increase the effectiveness of advertising campaigns.

All these features are designed to improve the user experience, increase engagement and make Twitter a more effective communication tool.

What is the difference according to AI between Twitter and Google?

Both Twitter and Google use AI in various ways to improve their services,
Bit the specific applications of AI and the emphasis on certain areas my differ between the two companies.

Twitter primarily uses AI for content curation and moderation, as well as to surface trending topics and create content. Twitter's AI algorithms are designed to personalize the user experience, help users discover content of interest, and keep the platform safe and appropriate.

Google, on the other hand, uses AI in a wider range of applications. Google's search engine, for example, uses AI to understand user queries and provide the most relevant results. Google also uses AI in its products such as Google Maps, Google Translate, Google Photos, and many more. Google also has a large research division focused on AI and its applications, which has led to the development of technologies such as TensorFlow, an open-source machine learning library.

In summary, while both companies use AI to improve their services, the specific applications and emphasis on certain areas may differ. Twitter primarily uses AI for content curation and moderation, while Google uses AI in a wider range of application such as search, language processing, and more.

How does Mark Zuckerberg use AI?

Mark Zuckerberg, the CEO of Facebook, has been actively exploring the use of AI to improve various aspects of the social media platform. Some examples of how Facebook is using AI include:

- **News feed curation:** AI algorithm are used to personalize the news feed for each user, showing them content that is most relevant to their interests.
- **Image and video recognition:** AI is used to automatically identify and tag people in photos and videos, making it easier for users to find and share content.
- **Language translation:** Facebook uses AI to automatically translate posts and comments into different languages, making the platform more accessible to a global audience.
- **Spam detection:** AI is used to identify and remove spam and fake accounts from the platform.
- **Advertising:** Facebook uses AI to optimize ad targeting and improve the performance of advertising campaigns.

Overall, AI is used in a variety of ways by Facebook to improve the user experience, increase engagement and make the platform more efficient.

Which education has Mark Zuckerberg?

Mark Zuckerberg is a college dropout, he attended Harvard University and studied computer science, psychology, and linguistics. He also took courses at the nearby Massachusetts Institute of Technology (MIT). He was known for his programming skills and created a number of popular applications while at Harvard, including the early version of Facebook, which was called "thefacebook" at the time.

In his sophomore year he wrote a program called Facemash,

which allowed students to compare the attractiveness of their classmates, this led to his disciplinary action and later on he dropped out of Harvard to focus on growing Facebook.

What is Metaverse?

The "metaverse" is a term used to describe a virtual reality space that is fully immersive and interactive, often used as a collective virtual shared space, created by the convergence of virtually enhanced physical reality and physically persistent virtual reality. It is a concept that has been popularized in science fiction, but is becoming more relevant as technology advances.

In the Metaverse, users can interact with each other and with virtual objects and environments using avatars, and can participate in a wide range of activities such as gaming, socializing, education, and commerce. The Metaverse is considered as a new digital frontier that will be accessible to anyone with internet connection and it's predicted to be the next big thing after the internet.

The Metaverse is a concept that is still in the early stages of development, and there is currently no single platform or technology that fully embodies it. However, many companies, such as Facebook and Google, are investing in VR and AR technologies and developing platforms that could eventually part of the Metaverse.

Will the Metaverse change our thinking?

It is possible that the Metaverse could change our thinking in a number of ways. Some of the ways in which it could impact our thinking include:

- **New forms of communication and collaboration:** The Metaverse could enable new forms of communication and collaboration, allowing people to interact with each other and with virtual objects and environments in ways that are not currently possible. This could change the way we think about social interactions and communication.

- **New forms of expression and creativity:** The Metaverse could enable new forms of expression and creativity, allowing people to create and share virtual experiences and objects that are not currently possible. This could change the way we think about art, design, and other creative fields.
- **New forms of learning and education:** The Metaverse could enable new forms of learning and education, allowing people to explore virtual worlds and participate in virtual simulations that are not currently possible. This could change the way we think about education and training.
- **New forms of commerce and economy:** The Metaverse could enable new forms of commerce and economy, allowing people to trade and exchange virtual goods and services that are not currently possible. This could change the way we think about business and commerce.

Overall, the Metaverse is expected to bring about a new way of thinking about the digital world and how we interact with it. It could change the way we think about how we communicate, learn, and interact with each other, as well as how we express ourselves and make a living.

We are sure that there will be a lot of challenges due to the new technologies with AI. I myself have been dealing with creative thinking for over 60 years, then you will still be able to do it. You can't avoid dealing with the matter anyway. Benefit from my experiences and insights!

YOU CAN DO 1,000 TIMES MORE THAN YOU KNOW

The tragedy of many people consists in believing throughout their lives that they can do less than others. More precisely: You would like to do something, but don't dare to do it and therefore refrain from doing it. One day when they are old, and maybe they are really old, they will mourn the missed opportunities.

This will now be completely different with the help of AI! Because everyone can explore and structure their wishes and ideas with AI and generate much more knowledge than is available in their brain, provided the right questions are asked. This is now possible in a dialog! A conversation with a machine that is constantly learning and knows more than anyone around you, including you. This idea may be frightening at first, but you simply learn a lot more about your tasks and can make decisions on a much broader basis.

What happens very often between desire and reality? A major barrier is the alleged head-hand discrepancy. The exaggerated distinction between theoreticians and practitioner will be less in the future. Of course, there are talents in both directions, but real talents are rare. It's just not true that thinking is reserved for the scientist.

When thinking we speak of the following chain: hypothesis, theory, principle, rule (strategy), concept, implementation.

Research in particular that leads to verified assumptions and ultimately to a theory, usually has very practical foundations. The unfortunate but constantly repeated thesis that theoreticians think better than practitioners must be recognized as absurd. People think differently, but the difference do not always have a qualitative dimension. It just depends on the problem.

Every craftsman has to think! When a carpenter builds a cabinet, a number of individual problems immediately arise that need to be considered. Already at the design stage, the shape, the style, the type of wood, the height, the width, the depth, the handle, the interior layout,
the feet, the lock and possible decorations must be considered. Through and with AI, the same craftsman can show his customer different cabinets beforehand. Not only that, he can also inform himself in detail about everything that is possible, across national borders and continents. About pieces of furniture that appear in films or in the homes of celebrities. Materials science and building instructions are also available.

I think a lot of autodidacts. Especially in art, with the hobbies and with restrictions even at work. The official path of education may be the only one for the masses, but everyone should realize that you can do better what you really like to do than what you don't like doing. There is no reason to think anyone can paint for yourself better than you can. Except that no one else would. It is utter nonsense to compete in everything we desire mentally. And then let it stay the same. How do we know what we can do if we haven't tried it? Nothing is as valuable in developing our skills as trying!

Uncertainty is always related to part of the past and to the entire future!

Which is easy to prove: What would have been ... if is uncertain! What will be ... is also uncertain! The present is much more decisive for our ability than the future. Of course, this fact is strongly disputed by some educators regarding the past and by all astrologers regarding the future. Nevertheless, I stick to it: The knowledge that we have forgotten or can- not apply is of little use for us. Only the knowledge we have at hand, also psychological, is useful. Experiences are of course useful, but experiences, even the wrong ones, are experienced as certain. And the future is in no way predictable, although belief in the predictions can be great. It doesn't change that: Predictions may or may not come true.

The present lasts just over two seconds! That's not a lot and you'd have to be pretty wide awake if you don't want to miss it. Of course, that's not always bad, because time happens continuously. You always get a new chance to react when circumstances don't change. What they do, however, often surprisingly!

How do past, present and future affect human thought?

The concept of past, present and future can affect human thought in a variety of ways. The past can influence our memories and beliefs, shaping our understanding of the world and influencing our decisions. The present can affect our perception of reality and our ability to focus on the task at hand. The future can influence our goals, aspirations, and expectations, guiding our decision-making and shaping our sense of purpose. Additionally, the way people think about time, whether they have a more present-focused or future-focused mindset can also affect their thoughts and behavior.

How does a strongly past-focused mindset affect thinking?

A strongly past-focused mindset, also known as a "past-negative" mindset, can affect thinking by causing an individual to dwell on negative experiences and regrets from the past, and may lead to feelings of sadness, depression, and low self-esteem. People with this mindset may have difficulty moving on from past traumas or negative experiences, which can make it hard for them fully enjoy the present moment and plan for the future. They may also be more likely to experience feelings of guilt, shame, or anger related to the past experience, which can affect their relationships and overall well-being. A strongly past-focused mindset may also lead to the difficulties in decision making, as the individual may be more likely to be influenced by the past regrets rather than focusing on the present or the future.

On the other hand, a strongly past-focused mindset can also be positive, if the individual is focused on the positive aspects of the past, it may lead to feelings of nostalgia, contentment, and an appreciation for the value of past experiences. They may be better able to learn from their past experiences and to use that knowledge to make better decisions in the present and future.

How does a strongly present-focused mindset affect thinking?

A strongly present-focused mindset, also known as a "present-hedonic" mindset, can affect thinking by causing an individual to prioritize immediate pleasure and satisfaction over long-term goals and plans. People with this mindset tend to be more impulsive, and may make decisions based on the potential for immediate rewards rather than considering the potential consequences of their actions. They may also be mor likely to engage in risky or unhealthy behaviors because they prioritize the present moment over the future. On the other hand, they may be more likely to enjoy and appreciate the present moment and to be less prone to worry or anxiety. However, a strongly present-focused mindset can also lead to difficulties in planning and achieving long-term goals, and may result in financial, professional or personal problems over time.

How does a strongly future-focused mindset affect thinking?

A strongly-future-focused mindset, also known as a "future-oriented" mindset, can affect thinking by causing an individual to prioritize long-term goals and plans over immediate pleasure and satisfaction. People with this mindset tend to be more self-disciplined, planful and persistent in pursuing their goals. They are less impulsive and more likely to make decisions based on their long-term goals and the potential consequences of their actions. They may also be more likely to engage in healthy and productive behavior, such as saving money, studying for exams, or working on a project, because they are focused on the future. However, a strongly future-focused mindset can also lead to difficulties in enjoying and appreciating the present moment, and may result in higher level of stress, anxiety or disappointment if future goals are not met. It can also lead to neglect of the present and the people in it.

What is the ideal human mindset?

The ideal human mindset is likely to be a balance of past, present, and future focus. It is important to learn from the past and use that knowledge to make informed decisions in the present, while also having a clear understanding of one's goals and aspirations for the future.

Having a balance mindset allows an individual to learn from their past experiences, appreciate and enjoy the present moment, and plan for the future. This mindset allows individuals to have a sense of purpose, a sense of perspective and also, the ability to manage stress, and make good decisions. Also, they are able to built and maintain healthy relationships, and are more likely to lead a happy and fulfilling life.

It's worth noting what may be the ideal mindset for one person may not be the same for another, as it depends on the individual's personality, goals, and life circumstances. It is important for each person to find what works for them and to make adjustments as needed.

How does AI change the ideal mindset?

AI has the potential to change the ideal human mindset in a number of ways. One way is by providing ne tools and technologies that can help people to better balance their focus on the past, present, and future. For example, AI-powered personal assistants or scheduling apps can help individuals to better manage their time and stay organized, which can make it easier for them to balance their focus on the present and future.

Another way that AI can change the ideal mindset is by providing new insights and information that can help individuals to make better decisions. For example, AI-powered analytics tools can help people to better understand their own behavior and the behavior of others, which can help them to make more informed decisions about their lives and career.

AI can also change the ideal mindset by providing new opportunities for people to learn and grow. For example, AI-powered educational tools can help people to learn new skills and gain new knowledge in a more efficient and personalized way.

It's worth noting that AI can also change the ideal mindset in a negative way. Over-reliance on AI to make decisions or to manage one's life can lead to a lack of critical thinking and problem-solving skills, and a reduction in the ability to manage stress and emotions. AI can also lead to a lack of privacy and security, which can cause negative emotions and stress. Therefore, it is important to use AI in a responsible and balanced way, and to be aware of its potential negative effects on the mindset.

What is the difference between critical and creative thinking?

Critical thinking is the process of analyzing and evaluating information in order to make a judgement or form a conclusion. It involves questioning assumptions, examining evidence, and considering alternative perspectives. Creative thinking, on the other hand, is the process of generating new and unique ideas. It involves thinking outside the box and coming up with original solutions to problems. While critical thinking is focused on evaluating and analyzing, creative thinking is focused on generating and imaging. Both skills are important for problem-solving and decision-making, but they are used in different ways and at different stages of the process.

The different ways and stages are:

Critical thinking is typically used in the early stages of problem-solving, when it is important to understand the problem at hand and evaluate the information that is available. It involves activities such as:

- **Defining the problem:** Understanding the question or challenge that needs to be addressed.
- **Gathering information:** Collecting data, facts, and evidence related to the problem.
- **Analyzing information:** Examining the information to identify patterns, relationships, and connections.
- **Evaluating information:** Assessing the credibility, relevance, and reliability of the information.
- **Making a judgement:** Drawing conclusions based on the information that has been analyzed and evaluated.

Creative thinking is used later in the problem-solving process, when it is
time to generate new ideas and solutions. It involves activities such as:

- **Brainstorming:** Generating a list of as many ideas as possible, without evaluating them.
- **Mind-mapping:** Creating a visual representation of the problem and possible solutions.
- **Free association:** Making connections between seemingly unrelated ideas.

Both critical and creative thinking are important for problem-solving and decision-making, but they are used indifferent ways at different stages of the process. Critical thinking helps to define the problem and evaluate information, while creative thinking helps to generate new ideas and find new solutions. Together, they can lead to more effective problem-solving and decision-making.

STRATEGIC THINKING WITH AI

Strategic thinking with AI can provide several advantages, including:

1. Improved decision-making: AI can analyze large amounts of data
   and identify patterns that humans may not be able to detect, allowing
   for more informed decisions.

2. Increased efficiency: AI can automate repetitive tasks and perform
   complex calculations quickly, allowing organizations to make faster
   decisions and respond to changes more effectively.

3. Enhanced forecasting: AI can use historical data to make predictions
   about future trends and events, allowing organizations to plan and
   prepare for potential outcomes.

4. Improved customer service: AI can be used to personalize customer
   interactions and provide more accurate and efficient service.

5. Better performance: AI can be used to optimize the performance of
   products, services and processes, helping organizations to gain

a

competitive edge.

Overall, strategic thinking with AI can help organizations to make better decisions, respond more quickly to chances, and gain a competitive edge in their industries.

How does that work in detail?

Strategic thinking with AI works by utilizing a range of AI techniques and tools to analyze large amounts of data and make predictions about future trends and events. This can involve several different steps, including:

1. Data collection: The first step is to collect and organize large amounts

of data from various sources, such as customer interactions, financial

transactions, or sensor readings.

2. Data preprocessing: The collected data is then cleaned and preprocessed to remove any errors or inconsistencies, and to ensure

that it is in a format that can be used for analysis.

3. Model training: Machine learning algorithms are then used to train

models on the preprocessed data. These models can be used for a

variety of tasks, such as image recognition, natural language processing, or predictive modeling.

4. Model evaluation: The trained models are then evaluated using a set

of test data to ensure that they are performing well and are able to

make accurate predictions.

5. Model deployment: Once the models have been evaluated,

they can
be deployed into production and used to make predictions and automate decisions in real-world situations.

6. Monitoring and updating: AI models need to be continuously monitored to ensure they are still performing well. This will include
updating the models with new data and retraining when necessary.

Overall, strategic thinking with AI works by collecting and analyzing
large amounts of data, training models to make predictions and
automate decisions, and deploying these models into production to
improve organizational performance.

Practical examples of strategic thinking with AI

One example of strategic thinking with AI is its use in supply chain management. Organizations can use AI to analyze data from various sources, such as sales data, inventory levels, and shipping schedules, to make predictions about future demand for products and identify potential bottlenecks in the supply chain.

For example, a retail company may use AI to analyze sales data to predict which products will be popular in the upcoming season. Using the information, the company can adjust its inventory level and shipping schedules to ensure that it has the right products in the right places at the right time.

Additionally, the company can use AI to monitor and optimize the performance of its logistic network, for example by routing deliveries to minimize transportation costs or reducing lead times.

Another example is the healthcare industry, where AI can be

used to analyze medical images, such as CT scans or MRI, to identify patterns or anomalies that could indicate a disease, allowing for more accurate and earlier diagnoses. This can have a significant impact on patient outcomes and can help to lower healthcare costs.

Overall, these examples show how organizations can use strategic thinking with AI to improve their performance by analyzing data, making predictions, and automatic decisions.

Are there any examples outside of business?

Yes, there are many examples of strategic thinking with AI outside of business. Here are a few:

1. Healthcare: AI can help healthcare professionals make more informed
   decisions by analyzing patient data and providing insight on treatment
   options. For example, AI algorithms can help doctors diagnose diseases
   more accurately or predict which patients are at higher risk of certain
   conditions.

2. Environmental Conservation: AI can be used to monitor and analyze
   environmental data, such as satellite imagery or weather patterns, to
   better understand the impact of human activity on the environment.
   This information can help policymakers make more informed decisions
   about environmental policies and conservation efforts.

3. Education: AI can help teachers and educational institutions
   personalize learning experiences for students by analyzing student data

and providing insights on learning preferences and progress. For
example, AI algorithms can recommend personalized learning plans or
identify areas where students need extra help.

How about important political decisions?

AI can potentially be used to inform and support important political decisions, but it is necessary to note that the use of AI in politics comes with its own set of ethical and social considerations.

One potential use of AI in politics is to analyze large amounts of data, such as public opinion polls, voting records, and social media activity, to identify patterns and trends that can inform policy decisions. For example, AI algorithms could be used to analyze social media sentiment around a particular policy proposal, helping politicians understand public opinion and tailor their messaging accordingly.

Another potential use of AI in politics is to predict the outcome of elections or referendums. By analyzing historical voting data and current polling information, AI algorithms can generate predictions on the likely outcome of an election. This information can help politicians make informed decisions about campaign strategy and resource allocation.

However, the use of AI in politics raises important questions around issues such as privacy, bias, and accountability. It is important to ensure that any AI systems used in politics are transparent and fair, and that they do not undermine the democratic process or violate individuals' rights. Ultimately, the use of AI in political decision-making should be approached with caution and with a focus on ensuring that it is used in a way that benefits society as a whole.

How does that look for the average citizen and his every day

life?

For the average citizen, the use of AI in strategic thinking can have a positive impact on their everyday life in several ways:

1. Personalized recommendations: AI can be used to analyze data
about an individual's preferences and behavior to make personalized
recommendations for products or services. For example, a music
streaming service may use AI to recommend songs or playlists based
on a user's listening history.

2. Improved customer service: AI can be used to provide more
accurate and efficient customer service, such as through chatbots or
virtual assistants. This can make it easier for individuals to get the
information or assistance they need.

3. More accurate and timely information: AI can be used to analyze
data from various sources to provide more accurate information to
citizens on time. For example, a weather forecasting service may
use AI to make more accurate predictions about weather patterns.

4. Automation of repetitive tasks: AI can be used to automate
repetitive tasks, such as scheduling appointments or paying bills, which
can save citizens time and effort.

5. Personalized healthcare: AI can be used to analyze medical data to
make personalized recommendations for healthcare. For

example, an

AI-based system can analyze an individual's medical history, lifestyle,

and genetic data to make personal recommendations for diet, exercise,

and medication.

Overall, the use of AI in strategic thinking can have a positive impact on the everyday lives of citizens by making it easier for them to access information, products, and services, and to automate repetitive tasks.

How can students benefit from AI?

Students can benefit from AI in several ways:

1. Personalized learning: AI can be used to analyze student data, such

as test scores and learning patterns, to create personalized learning

plans that are tailored to the individual student's needs and abilities.

2. Intelligent tutoring: AI-based tutoring systems can provide students

with personalized feedback and guidance, helping them to improve

their understanding of the material.

3. Automation of repetitive tasks: AI can be used to automate

repetitive tasks such as grading assignments, allowing educaters to

spend more time working with students.

4. Intelligent assessment: AI can be used to create more accurate and

efficient assessment, such as by automatically grading written responses or identifying patterns in student work.

5. Virtual reality and simulation: AI can be used to create immersive
  virtual reality and simulation experiences for students, which can help
  to make learning more engaging and interactive.

6. Intelligent search and retrieval: AI can be used to help students
  find and retrieve relevant information more quickly and easily by
  providing personalized search results.

Overall, AI can be a powerful tool for enhancing the student learning experience by providing personalized feedback, guidance, and assessment, as well as by automating repetitive tasks and making learning mor engaging and interactive.

How should homework be evaluated objective in the future?

On way to evaluate homework objectively in the future is to use computer-graded assessments, such as multiple choice of fill-in-the-blank questions. These types of assessments can be easily graded by a computer program, and the results can be immediately available to both the teacher and student. Another option is to use rubrics to evaluate homework, which provide clear and specific criteria for what is expected in the assignment. Rubrics can be used to evaluate both written work and projects, and they allow for consistent and objective evaluation. Additionally, using AI-based tools to grade homework and provide automated feedback to students can also be a way to make the process more objective.

The student's own creative output can no longer be evaluated when using AI, right?

Using AI to grade homework and provide automated feedback can be a useful tool, but it is important to keep in mind that AI may not be able to fully evaluate a student's creative output. AI can be used to assess certain aspects of a student's work, such as grammar and spelling, but may not be able to fully capture the nuances of a student's ideas or the originality of their thinking.

It's important to remember that AI systems are only as good as the data they are trained on, and if the data used to train the system does not include a wide range of examples of student work, the AI may not be able to accurately evaluate all types of student responses.

It's also important to consider that AI can be used to assist in the evaluation process, but it should not be the sole method of evaluation. Instead, teachers should use a combination of AI and human evaluation to provide a more comprehensive assessment of a student's work.

It is also important to keep in mind that creativity is subjective and hard to evaluate, so human teachers should always be involved in the evaluation process.

What are the advantages of using AI for me as a scientific author and for my readership?

As a scientific author:

1. AI can help with tasks such as language translation, making it easier to
   reach a wider audience.

2. AI tools can assist in data analysis and visualization, leading to more
   accurate and efficient research.

For your readership:

1. AI can also provide real-time information and updates, making the
   research more accessible and up-to-date.

2. AI can also provide interactive elements, making the research

more
engaging and accessible to a wider audience.

3. With the help of AI, it is possible to provide personalized
recommendations and insights based on the reader's interests and
preferences.

Of course, it is my goal as an author to provide as many readers with knowledge through the content. How can AI help me with this in detail?

AI's response in seconds:

AI can help you achieve your goal of providing knowledge to a large audience in several ways:

1. Text summarization: AI algorithms can generate summarized
versions of your scientific paper, making the content more easily
accessible and digestible for a wider audience.

2. Natural language processing: AI can help simplify complex scientific
terms and make the language more accessible to a non-expert reader.

3. Personalized recommendations: AI algorithms can provide
individualized content recommendations based on the reader's previous
interactions with the research, making it more relevant and engaging.

4. Interactive elements: AI can assist in the creation of interactive
figures, simulations, and visualizations, making the research more
engaging and accessible to a diverse audience.

5. Multilingual support: AI language translation models can
automatically translate your research into different languages, allowing
for wider distribution and reach.

Okay, what does that mean for the readership of my book?

1. Quick understanding: AI-powered text summarization can provide a
concise overview of the key points in your research, allowing readers to
quickly grasp the essence of the work.

2. Clarity of language: AI natural language processing can simplify
complex scientific terms and jargon, making the content accessible to a
wider audience.

3. Relevant recommendations: AI algorithms can provide personalized
recommendations based on the reader's interest and reading history,
guiding them to the most relevant information.

4. Engaging visualizations: AI-powered visualizations and simulations
can make the research more interactive and appealing, increasing
reader engagement and understanding.

5. Multilingual accessibility: With AI-powered language translation,
your research can reach a wider global audience, regardless of
language barriers.

6. Real-time updates: AI can provide real-time information and update

to your research, keeping the content current and relevant for a longer
period.

What additional tools are required to this?

To implement AI in your scientific research and book publishing, you would require the following tools:

1. Natural language processing (NLP) tools: These tools can be used
to simplify complex scientific terms, generate summaries, and perform
language translation.

2. Data analysis and visualization tools: These tools can be used to
analyze and visualize scientific data in a more engaging and interactive
manner.

3. Personalization tools: These tools can be used to provide
personalized recommendations and insights to the reader based on
their interests and reading history.

4. Machine learning platforms: These platforms can be used to train AI
algorithms on large datasets, allowing them to generate more accurate
and relevant results.

5. Development tools: Depending on the specific use case, you may also
require software development tools such as programming languages
(e.g. Python), libraries, and APIs to develop custom AI applications.

It is important to note that some AI tools may require significant computational resources, and you may need access to powerful hardware such as GPUs to train large machine learning models. Additionally, depending on the specific use case, you may require specialized expertise in the field of AI and machine learning.

If I understand everything correctly myself, then for me these are quite significant demands on my own knowledge. Well, so fare I have published 24 books in five different publishers not only on the subjects of "thinking"
and "creativity", but also on "management" and "psychology". I'm already excited, to see what I can achieve with and about AI!

What are the requirements for my readers?

The requirements for your readers (is the answer of AI) would depend on the context of your writing. In general, some common requirements for readers may include:

1. Ability to read and understand the language used in your writing

2. Basic knowledge or interest in the topic you are writing about

3. Attention and focus to comprehend the content of your writing

4. Access to any necessary technology or devices (such as a computer or
   mobile device) to view your writing.

It's important to consider your target audience and their background, needs, and expectations when writing to ensure that your writing is accessible and meets their requirements.

I write about how thinking is changing with AI and why it is necessary to use it. What are the arguments for this thesis?

1. Improved Efficiency: AI can automate many tasks, freeing up

time
and resources that can better used in other areas.

2. Increased Accuracy: AI can reduce the likelihood of errors, leading to
improved accuracy and better outcomes.

3. Better Insights: AI can analyze large amounts of data, identify patterns, and provide insights that would be difficult for humans to
uncover.

4. Enhanced Personalization: AI can provide personalized experiences
and recommendations, leading to better customer satisfaction.

5. Predictive Maintenance: AI can help predict when a machine or
system is likely to fail, reducing downtime and increasing productivity.

6. Improved Decision Making: AI can provide real-time data analysis
and decision-making support to humans, enabling them to make mor
informed decisions.

7. Cost Savings: AI can reduce costs associated with manual processes
and increase overall efficiency, leading to cost savings for organizations.

8. Competitive Advantage: Companies that adopt AI early can gain a
competitive advantage over their rivals and remain ahead of the curve.

In conclusion, the arguments for using AI in changing the

thinking process is that it leads to increased efficiency, accuracy, and decision-making capabilities, while also delivering cost savings and a competitive advantage.

As you can see, there are many arguments for using AI in business and private life in the future. There is no question that you personally benefit from it, especially if you ask your chatbot the right questions! From now on questions are more important than answers, so that you can expand your knowledge and make better decisions.

INVENT AND SOLVE PROBLEMS BEFORE THEY REALLY BECOME PROBLEMS

I know nobody cares what I wrote in 1982, but I can assure you that it was entirely without AI. And that's why it's especially valuable for some thoughts about thinking. But we had better assume what is possible in 2023 and the years to come, and that will be revolutionary in terms of our thinking.

Many people have gotten into the habit of taking the second step before the first, no wonder we stumble mentally and emotionally. In other words: We get in trouble!

Example 1:
So-called personal computers are offered on the market. For everyone. I'm not against computers, but I do suggest that before we buy a so-called personal computer, our own personal computer, our brain, shouldn't be made to think better. How so? The computer people said: Stupid people use the phone too!

(At the time I owned one of the earliest models of IBM PCs, which couldn't do any more than my IBM ball-head typewriter, but were 10 times more expensive. In any case, I was already familiar with critical thinking!)

Example 2:

You travel to distant countries by plane. I'm all for travelling. But shouldn't you get to know your own country first? How so? Said the tour operators: When it comes to the weather, you should play it save!

(At the time, I had consulting clients in a total of 25 different countries. Of course, there was no other way than to visit them by plane.)

Example 3:
You need your own apartment, even if you don't earn anything yet. How so? Ask the young people. The rooms with the parents may be nicer. But what are spaces compared to the dream of independence?

(At the time I had already started a family, there were two children and I had bought a house in a nice area with a large garden. Besides, it was the best investment I've ever made because the prices have gone through the roof in the prime location. Decisions also have to do with thinking!)

There were obviously worlds between what I wrote and what I consequently thought and my own reality. Very interesting, so we can have different opinions at the same time. The question is how that will play out when we use AI. Will we listen to what the chatbots tell us or not? Should we even? Some professors, journalists and students have tried to trick the AI and of course it's possible in this early phase. All you have to do is ask them which is heavier, a ton of steel or a ton of goose feather. But that will change with more practice.

I think we must first consider why we get into trouble when we think. For example, think in terms of claims instead of requirements and in automatic instead of active. All of our difficulties stem from a lack of information. Either we know how to little and don't know how to process the information we have, or we have the wrong information. This problem is supposed to be different now with AI, provided we use this tool and it's properly trained.

Thinking is not as simple a thing as we commonly think. Let's let the AI get to the main factors:

What is important for the thinking process and how does it work neurologically?

The thinking process is dependent on various factors, including:

1. Attention and focus: the ability to direct and sustain attention
   towards a task or thought.

2. Memory: the ability to store and recall information.

3. Problem-solving skills: the ability to analyze and find solutions to
   problems.

4. Language processing: the ability to understand and produce language.

5. Emotion regulation: the ability to understand and manage emotions.

Neurologically, the thinking process involves the activation of neural networks in the brain, specifically in the frontal and parietal lobes. This activation is regulated by neurotransmitters and is influenced by previous experiences and emotions. The thinking process is a complex, dynamic interaction between different brain regions.

That's a very good explanation from which we can learn something, but perhaps we should dig a little deeper.

Can the brain function when thinking be explained in more detail?

1. Neural activity: Thinking involves the activation of neurons in the

brain, creating electrical and chemical signals that are transmitted
between brain regions.

2. Brain regions: Different types of thinking are associated with the
activation of specific brain regions, such as the frontal lobe for

executive function, the temporal lobe for language processing, and the
parietal lobe for spatial reasoning.

3. Synaptic connections: Thinking also involves the strengthening or
weakening of connections between neurons, known as synaptic
plasticity, which allows for the storage and retrieval of information.

4. Neurotransmitters: The release of neurotransmitters, such as
dopamine and norepinephrine, modulates the activity of brain regions
and the transmission of signals between neurons, impacting the
efficiency of thinking.

5. Experience and learning: The brain's function during thinking is also
shaped by experience and learning, as repeated stimulation of neural
circuits can lead to the strengthening of specific connections and the
formation of new ones.

Overall, the brain's function during thinking is a complex and dynamic process that involves the coordination and integration of multiple brain regions and neurotransmitter systems.

When it comes to thinking, we rarely overestimate our abilities, and we don't judge our ourselves correctly, instead underestimating what we can achieve. In fact, if you think you have no ideas and you can't think of anything, you really have no ideas. Thinking, however, is not in itself a quantitative matter. The number of gray cells is quite comfortably sufficient for each and every one of us. What has significantly differentiated us in the past was first the knowledge and then the linking technique, which is called thinking outside the box. AI can increasingly take over this part in the future. Not complete and uncontrolled, but very helpful nonetheless.

Thesis: Your thinking must have a purpose!

Having a purpose for our thinking is important because it helps us stay focused and motivated, and it allows us to achieve our goals more effectively. When we have a clear purpose for our thinking, we can direct our thoughts and actions towards specific outcomes, and we can evaluate our progress and adjust our approach if necessary.

Here are a few reasons why having a purpose for our thinking is important:

1. Achieving goals: When we have a purpose for our thinking, we can
focus our thoughts and actions towards achieving specific goals. This
helps us stay motivated and make progress towards our desired
outcomes.

2. Prioritizing tasks: Having a clear purpose for our thinking can help us
prioritize our tasks and activities. We can focus on the most important
tasks first and work towards achieving our goals more

efficiently.

3. Making decisions: When we have a purpose for our thinking, we can
   make more informed and effective decisions. We can evaluate different
   options based on how well they align with our purpose, and choose the
   option that is most likely to help us achieve our goal.

4. Improving creativity: Having a clear purpose for our thinking can
   also improve our creativity. By focusing our thoughts and actions
   toward specific goal, we can generate new ideas and solutions that are
   more relevant and useful.

Overall, having a purpose for our thinking helps us be more effective, efficient and creative in achieving our goals. It allows us to stay focused and motivated and to make informed decisions that are more likely to lead to success.

INVENTING PROBLEMS IS THE SECRET OF SUCCESS

Contrary to what many people think, problems are very positive. Without problems there would be no solutions, and without solutions there are no problems. If we didn't have to earn our living, if we didn't have to worry about where to get food, housing, health, safety, sex, appreciation, recognition, knowledge, self-realization, we would definitely be doing badly.

Man needs problems like the air to breathe. He is the only creature that can see and solve complex problems. Of course, he longs not to have some troublesome problems, and he can not solve all problems at the same time. But if he didn't have one, he would immediately long to have some. He quickly finds boredom deadly. We store different templates for each unsolved issue over time: These patterns can be right or wrong. We can combine right parts with more information and forget wrong parts. This process is called experience.

Conversely, we can also forget correct patterns and store new, completely erroneous insights. The information does not have to come from outside, but can also come from within. Then we don't have to find someone to blame if they later turn out to be wrong. The more correct information we store, the more correct information we can logically combine. Actually, our natural storage is big enough, but the problem is not the limited capacity but the limited availability. Our memory is extremely limited, especially compared to the AI.

Without understanding the problem, any solution is random. Sometimes random solutions can turn into planned solutions that are based on structured approaches. But coincidences are rare. The more complex a problem is, the rarer it is. However, we are not concerned here with solving problems that anyone can easily solve, but with strategies and concepts for things that require a lot of knowledge. And – I'm consciously repeating myself – this is exactly what AI is made for.

Complexity of problems can lead to entanglement in details and, as we know, trigger fears in all areas of life. Fear is now pretty much the worst premise for humans to solve problems by means other than flight. In our densely populated and standardized world, escaping problems is not a tested means and recommended solution by just covering a distance. Or if one flees inwards, often with neurotic consequences. Or outwardly, not looking for the distance, but the hasty and ill-considered decision.

Complex problems, such as all social problems, from environmental pollution to unemployment, from the growth ideology to the housing shortage, are only possible by correcting the model of reality. Because reality is not a suitable indicator for future forecasts. But a snapshot. Using them as a basis for predictions is therefore as widespread as it is prone to error. The direction of tendencies can be determined much more accurately because they are dynamic scale developments and not static points. Anyone can see that AI can augment our ability to solve complex problems.

But we mustn't feel too sure: Unsolved problems often create new problems as well. However, not necessarily. Because there are definitely problems that actually solve themselves if you let them lie around long enough. For some, minor illnesses, for example, it can be extremely useful to wait a few days before going to the doctor. Because our body is constantly carrying out a self-healing process, repair work is being carried out without us noticing anything. The upper layer of our skin also renews itself in a few weeks, so we don't necessarily have to use that many expensive cosmetics for this.

We are used to solving problems in five main steps and call this systematic-logical approach:

1. Strategic formulation of the problem

2. Analysis and determination of the evaluation criteria

3. Alternative solutions (concepts)

4. Decision

5. Implementation

What is often not considered are the important areas of motivation and communication. It is precisely these sectors that have a direct impact of the quality of implementation. More precisely, on the design and the language.

I can now use AI's answer to demonstrate quite well how you can get a much more comprehensive answer to your question with the help of the chatbot. You can decide for yourself whether it will help you in your work and save you time!

What are the logical steps in the problem-solving process?

The problem-solving process typically consists of the following logical steps:

1. Identifying the problem: Define and understand the problem that
  needs to be solved.

2. Gathering information: Collect relevant information and data to help better understand the problem.

3. Developing possible solutions: Generate and consider a range of

potential solutions to the problem.

4. Evaluating solutions: Analyze the pros and cons of each potential
solution to determine the best course of action.

5. Choosing a solution: Select the most appropriate solution to
implement.

6. Implementing the solution: Put the chosen solution into action.

7. Monitoring progress: Continuously monitor and assess the
effectiveness of the solution, and make any necessary adjustments.

8. Refining the solution: Refine and improve the solution over time as
needed.

I think you can see quite well that it's not just about the eight instead of five points, not also about the content. By describing the individual steps in the problem solution more precisely, you can also improve the quality of the solution!

For decades I have seen my task as creating a counterweight in thinking that is beneficial to the cause. In other words, to introduce more biocybernetic system connections that are not so clearly regulated and fixed. And that are therefore by no means obvious. That's why I like to use words and visual signals to solve problems. Already in an early phase of the creative process, because philosophies and strategies consist of words. And in the conception phase, language plays at least an equally important role alongside the visual.

Words have the disadvantage of being abstractions of reality, but they also have the infinitely more important advantage of being not limited. They can be invented and assembled in unlimited numbers. I like neologisms and if it's allowed, one of my own examples is the term "info gaps" which I invented in 1984. The advantage of words is that they can say a lot in a very small space and are very specific. In my experience, it can be very useful to create a list of terms if you want to make it clear to yourself and others which ideas come into question.

For complicated. Problems, I don't just use a list, I formulate word diagrams. Because diagrams do not have to be limited to the graphic representation of numerical ratios. Even the non-technical person has the possibility, often without knowing it, of breaking down the stages of a problem-solving process into diagrams and thereby making them more transparent. Simple chain diagrams, which are practically the next level after the list, illustrate linear processes. However, problems are seldom so straightforward and usually more than one decision per stage is possible and necessary. That's why the tree diagram was invented. It is commonly referred to as a decision tree. Problem contexts can be shown quite well using decision trees. Because the yes/no consequences of complex problems do not always go as planned.

What are cybernetic system connections?

Cybernetic systems connections refer to the interactions and interconnections between various components of a system, including physical, computational, and human elements, to achieve a specific goal or set of goals. These connections allow the different parts of the system to communicate and exchange information, leading to coordinated and adaptive behavior. Cybernetic systems are commonly used in areas such as artificial intelligence, robotics, and control systems.

A practical example of a cybernetic system is a self-driving car. In this system, various components such as sensors, cameras, and actuators are connected to each other and to the car's control computer. The sensors gather information about the car's surroundings, the cameras capture images of the road ahead, and the actuators control the car's movements. All of these components are connected in a cybernetic system, allowing them to communicate and exchange information in real-time.

For example, the sensors may detect an obstacle in the road, and the control computer uses this information to direct the actuators to steer the care around the obstacle. The cameras also provide information to the control computer, which can use this information to confirm that the car is safely avoiding the obstacle. This type of interaction between the different components of the system is what makes the self-driving car a cybernetic system.

I think it's a very good explanation of a complicated thing that we've always wanted to know. Because such cars will soon be on the road, and of course the question arises of how safe they are and who is to blame if an accident occurs?

This is the AI's answer in February 2023!

Self-driving cars are still a relatively new technology, and the safety of these vehicles is an ongoing concern. The technology behind self-driving cars is designed to make driving safer, but accidents can still occur, just like with any other type of vehicle.

In terms of who is to blame if an accident occurs, it depends on the specific circumstances of the accident. If the accident was caused by the malfunction of the self-driving technology or a design flaw, then the manufacturer or designer of the technology could be held liable. If the accident was caused by human error, such as a person jumping in front of the self-driving car, then the person who caused the accident would be held responsible.

In some cases, it can be difficult to determine who is at fault in an accident involving a self-driving car. For example, if the self-driving technology failed to detect an obstacle, but a human driver in a traditional vehicle would have been able to see the obstacle and avoid it, then the manufacturer of the self-driving technology may be held liable.

As with any new technology, the safety of self-driving cars is a complex issue that will continue to evolve as the technology develops and becomes more widespread.

That too is a satisfactory explanation! Congratulations to the unknown bot! By the way – I'm a designer myself, but not in the technical field. If I imagine that it could be my fault if an accident happens, I have to say that it would not be a pleasant thought, especially since everyone knows what can happen on our roads when people are even racing, drinking alcohol and taking drugs. Not a particularly reassuring thought!

The problems we have to invent are not necessarily the problems themselves, but the problems of the problems. I would like at this point to coin a thesis that can notoriously be considered fundamental:

THE PROBLEM IS
NOT THE PROBLEM,

BUT THE CONSEQUENCES ARE

THE PROBLEM!

I'll give you an example: Anyone can age whiskey in oak casks for twelve years and bottle it. Provided you have enough capital, that's no problem at all. Rather, the problem is getting that whiskey to the man or woman after the 12 years. Even if it tasted as good as Chivas Regal or Johnnie Walker, you're not going to get rid of it for the same price. Why not? Because people don't buy whiskey, they by brand images and the feeling associated with the brand.

It is the same with all things. Solving problems is child's play compared to considering the consequences. Because consequences are future events, no one can predict the future. If you see the consequences as the real problem, you can narrow them down more easily than if you ignore them. Every solution to a problem has consequences, ether positive or negative. A solution to a problem that has no consequences is absolutely useless. After all, if a ship's leak was its problem and the sealing was of no consequences, the leak would not have been a problem.

THE NEW THINK METHOD WITH AI SUPPORT

With the new way of thinking, I basically assume, as decades before, that our life and consequently also our thinking does not proceed in a straight line but in waves. There are numerous examples for this thesis.

The flapping of a bird's wings takes place in wave movements, just like the growth of a child. The weather, the seasons, the tides of the oceans, also music, the vibrations of sound, our whole life follows this principle. Neither do we continually grow to our full size, nor do we continually age.

Even in what is probably the most epochal of all scientific findings, in Einstein's theory of relativity, we find indications against Euclid's geometry: The presence of gravitational fields causes a curvature of physical space. Even the economy follows the age-old mountain and valley principle. The economy with rising growth rates is always followed by a recession with a cooling off. Death follows life.

Our learning and thinking generally is subject to ups and downs. Sometimes we can learn and think better, sometimes worse. Some days we can think of a lot and other days nothing at all. This also underscores the thesis that represents our basis: The straight line, which does not occur in nature, is less suitable for thinking than the curve. It is not for nothing that we speak of brain convolutions, but also of intestinal loops, eyeballs, shoulders, elbows, corners of the mouth, lungs and heart-shaped, kidney-shaped, and bodily curves.

Let's ask the AI: What is the difference from linear thinking?

Linear thinking refers to a method of problem-solving that proceeds in a sequential, step-by-step manner from beginning to end. It assumes that events and processes occur in a straightforward and predictable way.

The difference from linear thinking would be non-linear thinking, which is a more flexible, complex and holistic approach to problem-solving that takes into account multiple variables and allows for unexpected connections and deviations. Non-linear thinking allows for multiple solutions to a problem and encourages creative and innovative thinking. People vastly underestimate the complexity and non-linearity of the human cognition processes.

It thus confirms what I have published for a long time and used it in practice, that the method of non-linear thinking is superior to linear thinking. Which begs the question: What are the major aspects and advantages of non-linear thinking?

Non-linear thinking refers to a thought process that doesn't follow a strict sequential or causal pattern, and instead jumps between different ideas and connections.

Advantages of non-linear thinking include:

1. Creativity: Non-linear thinking allows for the generation of novel and unique ideas.

2. Flexibility: It enables individuals to see things from multiple perspectives, making them more adaptable and able to handle complex and changing situations.

3. Problem solving: Non-linear thinking helps individuals tackle complex problems by considering multiple solutions and connections simultaneously.

4. Innovation: It encourages individuals to think outside of the box and come up with innovative solutions.

5. Complex understanding: Non-linear thinking enables individuals to understand complex systems and patterns.

Overall, non-linear thinking can lead to a more dynamic and flexible thought process, which can be beneficial in various aspects of life, including work, creativity, and problem solving.

Are there examples where AI can improve non-linear thinking?

Yes, AI can be used to enhance non-linear thinking in several ways:

1. Creativity: AI can be used to generate novel and unique ideas by combining information in unexpected ways and drawing connections between seemingly unrelated concepts.

2. Problem solving: AI algorithms can analyze large amounts of data and identify patterns and connections that a human might miss, leading to new and innovative solutions to complex problems.

3. Decision making: AI can assist in decision making by providing recommendations based on data analysis and machine learning models.

4. Innovation: AI can be used to identify new and innovative uses for existing technologies or materials by exploring their properties and potential applications in novel ways.

5. Knowledge discovery: AI can help in discovering new knowledge by analyzing vast amounts of information and uncovering patterns and connections that might not be immediately obvious.

AI is still limited in its ability to fully replicate the creativity and intuition of human non-linear thinking, but it can serve as a valuable tool for augmenting and enhancing human cognition.

Are there any specific examples?

Yes, here are a few specific examples of AI improving non-linear thinking:

1. Generative Art: AI algorithms can be used to generate unique and visually appealing artwork that can inspire human artists and designers.

2. Music composition: AI algorithms can be used to generate mew and original music by combining elements from various existing compositions or styles.

3. Medical diagnosis: AI algorithms can assist doctors in diagnosing complex medical conditions by analyzing patient data and identifying patterns and connections that might not be immediately obvious.

4. Financial modeling: AI algorithms can be used to analyze financial data and identify new and innovative investment strategies.

5. Marketing: AI algorithms can be used to analyze customer data and identify new and innovative ways to target and engage customers.

These are just a few examples of how AI can enhance non-linear thinking and lead to new and innovative solutions in various fields.

I think the statements confirm in an impressive way how AI can support us in our thoughts and actions. We can't prevent this new technology anyway and we shouldn't demonize it, but check it very carefully, word for word and picture for picture. The liberation of what was previously conceivable from the narrow limits of what was feasible is progress.

The idea, that if we broaden our basic-knowledge we could automatically think better will no longer be enough in the future. Because the duplication of something that already exists is, at the best, the dissemination of knowledge. But using AI is about a new dimension of knowledge now and in the future. Something, that, in addition to our minds, we can use almost immediately and quickly in dialogue. Is there anything against it?

Are there arguments against using AI in this case?

Yes, there are some arguments against using AI in the context of non-linear thinking:

1. Lack of human intuition: AI algorithms are limited by the data they are trained on and the algorithms used to analyze it. They lack the human intuition and creativity that is necessary for truly innovative and unique solutions.

2. Bias in data: If the data used to train AI algorithms is biased, then the solution generated by the algorithms may be also be biased. This can be a major concern in fields where the consequences of bias can be significant, such as in healthcare or criminal justice.

3. Limitations in understanding: AI algorithms may not fully understand the context or meaning behind the data they are analyzing, leading to flawed solutions.

4. Dependence on data: AI solutions are dependent on the quality and availability of data, and may not be useful in cases where the necessary
Data is not available.

5. Ethical concerns: There are also ethical concerns around the use of AI in non-linear thinking, such as the potential for AI to automate certain jobs and displace human workers, or the use of AI for malicious purposes.

Overall, while AI can be a valuable tool for enhancing non-linear thinking, it is important to be aware of its limitations and potential downsides, and to use it in a responsible and ethical manner.

I myself made my decision and as everyone can see I used AI for this book. Of course, not without mentioning the critical points and checking the output. I expressly respect any other opinion, but based on the facts I think it is reasonable to include the new tool in my thinking because it can make an important contribution.

The simplest level of non-linear thinking is why thinking. It's easy for you to remember, because the question mark shows visually that you shouldn't think directly, but rather around the corner. If you ask yourself or the AI questions, then these should not only be questions that answer themselves, but also questions whose answers you don't know. But the AI rather than not, likely most of the time.

Prompt design basics

A prompt is a cue or stimulus that is used to help people think, recall information, or make decisions. Prompts can come in the form of a question, an image, a statement, or a sound. Prompts are often used in educational and therapeutic settings to help people understand and process information, or to help them recall something they have forgotten. For example, a teacher may give a prompt in the form of a question to help students think more deeply about a topic.

The quality of the input determines the output. Use plain language! The AI models can do everything from generating original stories to performing complex text analysis. Because they can do so many things, you have to be explicit in describing what you want. Showing, not just telling, is often the secret of a good prompt.

There are three basic guidelines to creating prompts:

Show and tell. Make it clear what you want either trough instructions, examples, or a combination of the two. If you want the model to rank a list of items in alphabetical order or to classify a paragraph by sentiment, show it that's what you want.

Provide quality data. If you're trying to build a classifier or get the model to follow a pattern, make sure that there are enough examples. Be sure to proofread your examples – the model is usually smart enough to see through basic spelling mistakes and give you a response, but it also might assume this is intentional and it can affect the response.

Check your settings. The temperature and top_p setting control how deterministic the model is in generating a response. If you're asking it for a response where there's only one right answer, then you'd want to set these lower. If you're looking for more diverse responses, then you might want to set them higher. The number one mistake people use with these settings is assuming that they're "cleverness" or "creativity" controls.

What is P-Setting? Well, because I'm not a griller and therefore don't own a grill, I couldn't know what is meant by a p-setting, but if a understood the matter correctly, old grills are equipped with 5 P settings. The P stands for pause. In case anyone is interested, a higher p-setting is good for high outside temperatures to prevent the grill from getting too hot.
This is also the case with a text model when it is overwhelmed by vaguely formulated questions. It is really crucial to be very precise in the language and content of the questions, which is practically only possible in areas that you are very familiar with.

For as long as there have been people, they have tried to make each other believe that straight-line thinking would lead straight to the desired success, because it connects problem A with solution B in the shortest possible way. This consideration is based on the historical knowledge that straight arrows fly better than crooked ones. We just often refuse to get the curve of rethinking. Thoughts are not arrows! While arrows are something artificial, thoughts are something natural. Everyone will agree that there is a diametrical difference between art and nature.

What is the difference between art and nature?

The main difference between art and nature is that art is a creation of human beings, while nature is a natural phenomenon that has not been crated or manipulated by humans. Art is an expression of creativity, while nature is a reflection of the natural world. Art is often used to interpret and express emotion, while nature is often used to inspire and provide a sense of peace. Art usually requires a conscious effort to create, while nature is simply a part of the environment that exists without any human intervention.

As we hopefully all know by now, climate change is due to human encroachment on nature, showing us that we need to be careful with nature if the earth is to remain habitable for future generations. At the moment, I think that moving to other planets like Mars is only possible for a limited number of people at best. Anyway, given the distances and living conditions there, I'm not as optimistic as other people with missile companies.

Living conditions on Mars are challenging, to say the least. Due to the planet's thin atmosphere, the atmospheric pressure is much lower than on Earth, and the temperatures can range from -195° F (-125° C) to 70° F (20° C). Additionally, the planets gravity is just 38% of Earth's, so living on Mars would require some adjustments to accommodate the lower gravity. Low gravity can have a number of impacts on the human body. In particular, it can cause muscle and bone loss, as well as changes in cardiovascular and respiratory systems. It also can lead to problems with balance and coordination, increased risk of dizziness, nausea and vomiting, and a weakened immune system. Long-term exposure to low gravity can also lead to vision problems, increased fatigue, and increased risk of infection. It is important to note that the effect of low gravity can be reversed with time spent in normal gravity.

Currently, it is not possible to artificially create gravity. Gravity is a natural phenomenon that is produced by the presence of mass and is inversely proportional to the square of the distance between to objects. Attempts have been made to create artificial gravity, but these have been largely unsuccessful due to the immense amount of energy required to generate gravity that is strong enough to have an effect on objects. However, some research is being done into the possibility of creating artificial gravity in space, such as by spinning a spacecraft or station.

A flight to Mars would take approximately 6 to 9 months, depending on the route taken and the speed of the spacecraft. Next to Earth, mars is the most habitable location in the solar system by terrestrial standards. Unfortunately, sending astronauts to Mars will inevitably entail a number of distinct challenges. Launch windows only occur every two years, when our planets are at the closest in their orbits to each other. Some problems are the flight trajectory and corrective maneuvers, the fuel management, the radiation, microgravity and health, the isolation and psychological issues, the communication, and the Mars approach and orbital insertion.

There are no straight lines in the nature

Actually, it should give us food for thought when we learn that aging does not proceed in a straight line, but also in curves. Just like the water doesn't flow straight ahead and the sky arches above us. Irregularity is more humane than regularity, which is why there has also been a new way of thinking in architecture. Straightforward thinking is technocratic thinking. Square meters, cubic meters of enclosed space, flat roofs – there was to much thought in straight lines. They not only lower the architectural level, but also the costs. You get more living space for less, bit less quality of life.

The structural mistakes can be seen in many satellite towns all over the world, and if you look more closely, the social consequences as well. The straight line is also the dividing line between black and white, which leads to silly black and white thinking. It is the exaggeratedly hard dichotomy of right and wrong, with the well-known consequences and persecutions of those who think differently.

To prove that it is not that easy to escape from box thinking, here is a very simple experiment!

You only need to solve this task:

8 5 4 9 1 7 6 3 2

According to what aspects are these nine digits arranged?

Certainly not a problem for you as a mathematically gifted person. Immediately you will probably start to calculate, add and subtract ... and get no result. Because as soon as we see numbers, we think we have to calculate. We simply have this impulse from our school days and this is an example of pronounced box thinking This task cannot be solved by straight-line thinking and therefore I want to set you a second task.

E J O T

What does this term mean?

Immediately you will use your language skills, maybe even the Bible story. Because when we see words, we want to grasp their meaning. Most of the time this way is correct, but in this case, it is exceptionally not.

Here is the very simple solution:

1. The series of numbers is arranged in alphabetical order!

2. The artificial word "EJOT" was created by putting the 5th, the 10th, the

15th and the 20th letter of the alphabet together!

What do these two small and simple experiments show?

A whole lot about our thinking: We are used to think in linear and straight lines! That is why we often fail to solve complex problems. Numbers have to have as little to do with mathematics as letters have with word meanings. When solving problems, the result of which we do not know, we cannot get any further with one-sided and technocratic thinking.

Out of curiosity and interest, I asked AI: According to what aspects are the digits 854917632 arranged?

The first answer: The digits 854917632 are arranged based on their numerical values in increasing order – was wrong! I tried several more times to get a correct answer, but obviously in February 2023 the AI could not recognize the solution in this case. It asked politely for more information, which would already have been the solution. On the one hand, this shows the limitations of AI at the time, but on the other hand this does not mean that the chatbot cannot present a result today. Developments in this area are proceeding very quickly!

What if we have a problem?

In any case, if we have a problem, a conflict scenario immediately arises. Because between the problem and the solution there is an obstacle and thus a bottleneck. Without obstacles there are no problems and therefore it is positive when we can see the obstacle. However, humans normally do not like to jump over obstacles and neither do horses as flight animals. If the bottleneck becomes an insurmountable wall, only aggression or resignation remains. Both have the same causes and triggers. Only the right thinking is suitable and overcoming bottlenecks.

Bottlenecks that are not overcome in a certain time, which can be a few minutes or several years, depending on the complexity, tend to close by themselves. As a result, the obstacle does not disappear, but it often grows. Or it dissolves because it wasn't anything worth thinking about.

When the solution to the problem is a very flat obstacle, we call it a simple task. Most people prefer to set themselves routine tasks that they already know how to solve and do not need additional AI for them. When problem, obstacle and solution are on one level, anyone can step over them without thinking and get on with the agenda.

On the other hand, in order to solve a difficult problem, an edge, a threshold, a corner, i.e. an obstacle, must always overcome, because without an obstacle there is no real problem. And if there is no problem, there is no solution. As soon as the solution radius is more than 180 degrees, i.e. a mental departure from what has already been learned, so to speak, normative solutions work less and less. In extreme cases, when the problem and the solution are diametrically opposed, i.e. the radius of the solution can reach 360 degrees and the obstacle is therefore the greatest, you have to think outside the box most of the time.

In the case of complex problems, such as those presented by large-scale projects, regardless of whether they concern architecture, corporate marketing strategies, or transport, social, or military planning, one is always faced with a labyrinth at first. This labyrinth does not consist of corridors of the same width that lead more or less straight to the goal. Rather, such labyrinths are a chain of very different cliffs, the radii of solution of which maliciously all exceed 180 degrees.

The order of the individual solution steps, which we usually call priority, can change in the course of the work, as can their number and degree of difficulty. For this reason, these projects also tend to become drastically more expensive over time. Complicated solutions are usually due to solutions that go over 360 degrees. Actually, the aim should be not to let the solution radius go over more than a full circle, but to divide it into as many steps as possible and necessary, but not to overdo it. The solution path of complicated solutions often looks like a turbulence, because individual steps occur unexpectedly, even though they are absolutely identical. This should be avoided, because otherwise the process can be confusing for those involved.

What are the benefits of using AI for problem-solving?

Some of the most common applications of AI for problem-solving in different industries include: Healthcare, Law, Finance, Retail, Transportation, Manufacturing. AI is revolutionizing these industries by making it more efficient and predict trends and discover patterns in data.
This helps making better decisions and to minimize risks. It is not yet possible to foresee what changes and chances AI will offer in the future. Experts are convinced that there will be major upheavals in almost all areas. The technology is just beginning, but it makes sense to use the situation to understand the next steps.

The next steps in the development of AI involve further research into algorithms and techniques to improve AI performance and methods to apply it to a variety of tasks. Additionally, it is important to focus on developing AI applications that are ethical and beneficial to both businesses and society as a whole. Finally, further research and development into AI technologies and applications, such as natural language processing, computer vision, and robotics, to ensure that AI is used responsibly and effectively.

What are good questions to ask about AI?

- What are the potential applications of AI?
- How is AI currently being used in different industries?

- What ethical considerations should be taken into account?
- What are the potential implications of AI in society?
- How can we ensure AI is developed in a responsible manner?
- What are the main challenges associated with AI development?
- How can AI be used to create positive outcomes for the world?

Your chatbot, whatever it's called, will give you an answer to your questions. If it is not precise enough for you, you can ask again. You have to decide for yourself whether they are true or not!

MORE SENSIBLE
THINKING THEORIES

As a creative director in international agencies and later also in my own agency, I also had a lot to do with big, well-known brands and world-famous trading companies that needed new ideas. That's why I've kept myself up to date with the latest developments in creative thinking over the three decades that I've been doing this job. And I've also thought about further possibilities of brainstorming and decision theory myself and have published scientific papers in this area. In this respect, I was not particularly surprised that with AI there is now a tool available that enables everyone to produce ideas in text and art at a much higher level than was previously possible.

Once the algorithms were able to distinguish between cats and dogs, the only thing that mattered the huge amount of data until they could recognize almost everything. Just not always the difference between good and bad. But it will probably happen soon!

Thinking big first can often be better than thinking straight to the point, with one exception. When you are in a conversation, you should direct your thoughts as precisely as possible to the topic. Otherwise, language becomes redundant. We all know when politicians and diplomats say something, but we really shouldn't assume that when we try to solve our own problems. Or the problems of our customers.

Encirclement Thinking

Large-scale thinking, I have called "encirclement thinking". In German "Einkreisungsdenken", in French "pensée d'encerclement", in Spanish „pensamiento de cerco" or in Portugués "pensamento cerco". The eagle also circles in the air for a long time before finally catching its prey with almost deadly certainty. This thinking and behavior are quite common in nature. I can come up with a creative name for the method if wanted: EAGLE CIRCLE (EC).

Maybe you can remember things better that way. In any case, the method offers the advantage of ventilating many aspects before you get to the point i.e. to the actual problem. It should be clear that encirclement thinking uses more stored patterns from the fringes to solve than immediately believing the first solution is the best. Direct control inevitably reduces possible alternatives. However, there is always one best solution and usually several other ones. Because the odds of coming up with less good solutions than the best at first are usually greater than the other way around. It's a good idea to occasionally adopt the eagle's position to look at things.

The Overshoot Method

Maybe I should come up with a brand name for this method, too, but first I'll explain it. In order to release thought patterns that are new in the combination, a liberating joke, conscious exaggeration, just overshooting a goal, is often a very effective method of ultimately coming up with suitable ideas for a solution. Everyone will immediately understand that a bitten apple is an insanely good idea to label a technical product. You just have to dare to overshoot the target.

The higher and more difficult the targets are, the greater the uncertainty when it comes to hitting the target, because distant opportunities are naturally the last to be seen. By consciously overshooting the target, the hidden ideas have a chance to be included in the thinking and not forgotten. By the way, one should always remind oneself – we generally laugh at what we consider to be wrong because it does not correspond to our basic understanding.

The integration of nonsense makes perfect sense. It promotes creativity in a sustainable way. It is interesting to note that those who consciously think nonsense for the purpose of solving problems almost never actually do great nonsense and do damage. Whereas nonsensical acts are mostly committed by those who did not consider their thinking nonsense at the time of the act. Our attention-seeking society constantly expects new crazy ideas from users, and as is well known, this is also part of the business model of the so-called social networks, which with they earn their money.

As can often be observed, children like to do nonsense and very consciously. Already in kindergarten and later the massively in school, not only behavioral nonsense, but also thinking nonsense is suppressed. This orientation towards supposedly meaningful thinking, which is often misconstrued as logical thinking, only promotes sterility in thinking. As a result, there are fare too few adults today who can consciously overshoot the mark in their thinking. Thinking around the corner means moving away from the center. Because, as is to be expected, mediocrity-oriented thinking takes place predominantly and frequently in the middle. But the new thinking takes place on the fringes, while in the middle very spongy and worn-out thinking is the rule. They come from the edge: the new and fresh ideas, the sensational new art, the unfinished approaches!

Highly flexible thinking

One can speak of flexibility in thinking when a small amount of new information of the same quality is sufficient to beat a larger amount of stored old information.

My thesis: Thinking is all the more flexible the greater the quantitative difference between new information and old

information that results in a change in opinion.

The extreme of flexibility in thinking is when a single piece of new information can make all stored sensory impressions, which can be thousands, become obsolete. The 180-degree turnaround in opinion-forming is by no means always a sign of fickleness, but sometimes also of intelligence. In order to overcome problem hurdles, not as many patterns are needed as are already stored, but only better ones. This realization has incredibly positive effects on the time available, which is always extremely limited. Because time is the only thing we cannot produce. That's why it is much more valuable than money.

And in case you are interested: I already formulated this thesis and explanation in 1982, when there was neither the Internet nor AI. It is still valid word for word! But it is much more important what opportunities arise from this scientific knowledge today, more than 40 years later? Now with the use of artificial intelligence?

Maybe we should ask one of the many chatbots!

What makes thinking more flexible?

Several factors can contribute to making thinking more flexible, including:

1. Embracing diversity and multiple perspectives. By exposing yourself to different opinions, beliefs, and experiences, you can broaden your thinking and become more flexible.

2. Keeping an open mind. Being open to new ideas and considering
    alternative ways of doing things can help you adapt to new situations
    and make more informed decisions.

3. Challenging assumptions and biases. Being aware of your own

biases and assumptions can help you recognize when thinking is
inflexible, and challenge them in a constructive way.

4. Developing critical thinking skills. By learning how to analyze
information, evaluate arguments, and draw conclusions based on
evidence, you can become a more flexible thinker.

5. Engaging in mental exercises. Practices such as brainstorming,
visualization, and mind mapping can help you approach problems from
different angles and generate new ideas.

6. Practicing mindfulness and emotional regulation. Mindfulness and
emotional regulation can help you stay focused, manage stress, and
maintain perspective, which can all contribute to flexible thinking.

Has the quantitative difference between new information and old information an effect on opinion?

Yes, the quantity of new information can have an effect on opinion. People tend to form opinions based on the information that is readily available to them, and a larger quantity of new information can alter their opinion by exposing them to different perspectives, facts, and evidence.

However, it's important to note that the quality of the information is also crucial. Just because there is a large quantity of information does not necessarily mean that it is credible, accurate, or relevant. People may also have their own biases and preconceptions that can influence the way they process and interpret information, regardless of the quantity.

Ultimately, the effect of new information on opinion is complex and can depend on a variety of factors, including the individual's existing beliefs, the sources of the information, and how it is presented and communicated.

What influences the formation of opinion particularly strong?

There are several factors that can influence the formation of opinion strongly, including:

1. Personal experience: People are more likely to form strong opinions

based on their own personal experiences and observations.

2. Emotion: Emotional responses to events and issues can have a strong

influence on opinions. People may feel passionately about a topic and

form strong opinions based on their feelings.

3. Social and cultural norms: People tend to conform to the opinions of

those around them, especially those they perceive as being similar to

themselves. Social and cultural norms can strongly influence opinion

formation.

4. Credible sources: People are more likely to form strong opinions if

they perceive the received information to be credible and trustworthy.

5. Confirmation bias: People tend to seek out in information that

support their existing opinions and beliefs, and ignore or dismiss

information that contradicts them. This can reinforce and

strengthen
existing opinions.

6. Information overload: Too much information can lead to confusion, and people may form strong opinions based on the first information they receive or the information that is easiest to understand.

It's important to note that these factors can interact and interact with each other in complex ways, and that opinion formation is influenced by a multitude of factors, including individual personality, background, and values.

In what ways will AI influence opinion?

Artificial Intelligence (AI) has the potential to influence opinion in several ways:

1. Information dissemination: AI algorithms are increasingly being
used to recommend content and filter information, which can shape the
information people receive and potentially influence their opinions.

2. Personalization: AI algorithms can be used to personalize information
and advertising, tailoring it to individual preferences and interests. This
can lead to people being exposed to more information that supports
their existing opinions and biases, potentially reinforcing those
opinions.

3. Automated decision-making: AI systems are being used to make
decisions in various industries, including criminal justice and finance,

which can influence public opinion about the fairness and reliability of
these systems.

4. Chatbots and fake news: AI-powered chatbots and deepfake technology
can be used to spread false information and manipulate public opinion.

5. Manipulation and influence: AI algorithms can be used for political
and commercial gain, for example, by automating the targeting and
delivery of political advertising to specific demographic groups.

It's important to note that AI can also be used to counteract the spread of misinformation and promote media literacy, and that the impact of AI on opinion will depend on how it is developed, deployed, and regulated. The responsible use of AI in shaping public opinion is a critical issue, and one that will require ongoing public debate and regulation.

Somersault thinking

Dealing with complexity is like swimming in the middle of the ocean for humans. Suddenly the weather changes and with it the situation. Adapting to such relatively rapid changes in complex systems can be very difficult. Only people who think highly of their abilities keep challenging themselves. It is sometimes difficult to use a principle of thought that deviates from everyday thinking. Deviating from the usual path is the whole secret of great art. And the deviation from everyday thinking is the secret of creative thinking.

The double to multiple circling around the same problem I have called somersault thinking. It is characterized by constant departures from just formulated opinions and changes of opinion without recognizable reasons. In business, somersault thinking often leads to difficulties because it is precisely corporate images and brand images that are least suited to a zigzag course. This wrong approach happens more often than thought and not only when there is a change of top management that wants to do everything differently.

What is somersault thinking?

As an AI language model, I'm not familiar with the term "somersault thinking". However, based on my understanding of the words, I would interpret it as a type of thinking that involves rapid and agile mental maneuvers, much like the physical acrobats of a somersault. Perhaps it refers to a way of thinking that involves quickly flipping through the air. It might suggest a type of thinking that is creative, playful, and flexible able to adapt to changing situations and find new solutions to problems.

What are the pros and cons of constantly changing opinions?

Constantly changing opinions can have both pros and cons, depending on the context and circumstances. Here are a few potential advantages and drawbacks:

Pros:

1. **Open-mindedness:** Constantly changing opinions can demonstrate a
   willingness to consider new information and viewpoints. This can be
   valuable trait in many settings, such as in scientific research or political
   decision-making.

2. **Growth and development:** Changing opinions can also indicate
   personal growth and development. As individuals gain new experiences

and knowledge, their opinion may naturally shift over time.

3. Flexibility: Being open to changing opinions can allow individuals to be
more flexible and adaptable, which can be useful in fast-paced or
uncertain environments.

Cons:

1. Inconsistency: Constantly changing opinions can make it difficult to
establish trust or credibility with others. People may perceive the
individual as being indecisive or lacking conviction.

2. Impressionability: Changing opinions to easily or frequently may
suggest that an individual is easily swayed by others, rather than
forming their own independent thoughts and ideas.

3. Lack of direction: If opinions are constantly changing, it may be
challenging to set and achieve long-term goals or make meaningful
progress in a particular direction.

Overall, it's important to strike a balance between being open to new ideas and perspectives while also maintaining a strong sense of personal values and beliefs. Consistently changing opinions should be done thoughtfully, with a clear understanding of the potential consequences and impact on ourself and others.

FROM THEORY TO PRACTICE AND BACK

What is the difference of theory and practice?

Theory and practice are two related but distinct concepts.

Theory refers to a set of principles, concepts, or ideas that explain a particular phenomenon or field of knowledge. Theories are often based on research, experimentation, or observation and are used to explain how things work or why things happen in a certain way. They can provide a framework for understanding and making predictions about the world.

Practice, on the other hand, refers to the application of theory in real-world situations. It involves using knowledge, skills, and techniques to accomplish a task or achieve a goal. Practice can involve experimentation, trial and error, and adaption in response to changing circumstances.

The difference between theory and practice is that theory is more abstract and conceptual, while practice is more concrete and hands-on. Theory can provide a foundation for understanding and guiding practice, but it is not always a perfect match with the reality of the situation. In some cases, there may be gaps or inconsistencies between theory and practice, and the practical application of a theory may require adjustments or modifications to make it work in a particular context.

All new projects, if they are to be completed successfully, always proceed in these four phases:

1. **Philosophy**

2. **Strategy**

3. **Conception**

4. **Implementation**

On the one hand, this is easy to remember, but it sounds somewhat difficult to understand because of the scientific terms. To make it a little easier, I have included the explanations.

Philosophy – striving for knowledge of the connections of things in the world

Strategy – planned action by setting a goal

Conception – artistic or technical idea, draft of a work

Implementation – realization, the way of execution

The quality of success of all our actions depends on the diligence of our thinking and acting in these four phases. Their order is fixed and should not be changed. However, what definitely makes sense is that in the future, by using AI and asking the right questions, we should be able to pick up important cues in formulation and execution across all four phases. Especially when it comes to complex problems.

I would like to explain these abstract thoughts to you by means of an example which is simple at first glance, but which has great significance for our lives. It is about our nutrition, a subject to which everyone has access because everyone likes to eat. The very word "likes to eat" carries with it the misunderstanding that this refers to quantity, which is of course absurd.

Imagine you not only have a kitchen, but you even want to cook in it, or you are thinking of opening a restaurant. Then, of course, you need a cooking philosophy! Well, there are more chefs with a price-quantity philosophy you don't want to copy. Those horrible large portions of cheap stuff at prices that are accepted by the masses. Fast food restaurants around the world show every day that this kind of thing can work. But it has also contributed to making around two-thirds of adult in industrialized countries overweight.

If we strive to see the interconnectedness of the world, which AI can help us with, we may come to realize that shoveling in relatively large amounts of relatively tasteless food con not only hinder weight gain, but can also be detrimental to health. It is a connection known for millennia, called food culture, but has not yet reached the brains of many eaters and cooks. One could think, if one wants to cook something tasty, to say: I want to offer only dishes in which I apply all my knowledge about digestibility. If one had this philosophy, quantity thinking would inevitable be eliminated. Less, but better!

The following strategy could then be very well based on such a kitchen philosophy as described:

I want to offer the most flavorful, wholesome and varied dishes that can be produced at acceptable prices. To achieve this goal, the portions must be properly sized and consists exclusively on ingredients of the highest quality and freshness. The must also be prepared in a way that preserves vitamins.

There will be those who believe that such a strategy cannot be implemented on a broad basis. But that is fundamentally wrong; there are internationally enough examples where it succeeds. It's not about partridge paté and truffles, not lobster and Chablis. Nor is this example about kitchens and cooking alone, but for all things in life. A concept based on a strategy is fundamentally decisive. My conception here, as far as our food is concerned, is that less is more. It doesn't have to be anything rare or expensive! Imagination outweighs a lot of money in the kitchen, and not only there.

Picasso did not pay more for his paints than any amateur painter. The difference lies solely in the result. You have to use fresh, as natural as possible products. If more people did it, procurement would not be a problem at all, because more would be offered. I helped to create a natural food brand 40 years ago and formulated the slogan: Sensible for people and the earth! That's why I know what organic farming is and why it's better for people, animals and the climate.

For the conception I would like to give still some suggestions, which have to do with the practice:

As is well known, there are salads in all variations. Enriched with nutritious ingredients such as chicken, tuna, shrimp, rice, pasta, dressings, crème fraiche, cheese, ham and various vegetables. They can certainly replace a real lunch with several courses. There really are no limits to your imagination when cooking!

You see, we have imperceptibly already advanced to the 4th phase, the implementation. A chef may have the greatest ambitions, but if he is sloppy in the implementation, i.e. the preparation, everything is for nothing.

Theoretical thinking succeeds relatively many people quite excellently. Their goals may sometimes not be well thought out, but they usually have some and can also name them. From an early age, we are used to giving answers to questions about what we want. We can express very early whether we are hungry or thirsty.

Formulating what we want to have has a lasting effect on our thinking. This is because it is controlled by motivations, and this is an effective control from which it is difficult to escape as an individual only by sublimation or repression. Which can both be substitute actions that are often experienced unsatisfactorily.

People with a pronounced education generally know quite well what they want in life. Only they reach this goal less often than they imagine! This can be because the philosophies and strategies are already unrealistic. The tenfold more frequent reason, however, why our plans do not develop as desired, is due to serious deficiencies in the conception and implementation phase. This is the transition from theory to practice and realization.

In the future, it can be assumed that philosophies, strategies, conceptions and implementations can be worked out much more precisely through the use of AI. Of course, this is only possible if they are used appropriately and equipped with the right questions. That's exactly what I did!

What should be the philosophy, strategy, design and implementation for a good restaurant?

A good restaurant should have a well-designed philosophy, strategy, design, and implementation to succeed.

Philosophy: The restaurant's philosophy should reflect its core values and mission. It should provide a clear and concise explanation of what the restaurant represents and what it aims to achieve. This can include the type of cuisine it serves, the level of service it provides, and its overall atmosphere.

Strategy: The restaurant's strategy should take into account its target market, competition, and financial goals. It should outline the steps the restaurant will take to achieve its objectives, such as menu development, marketing, and customer service.

Design: The design of a restaurant is important as it sets the tone and atmosphere for the dining experience. This includes the layout of the space, the selection of furniture, and décor, and the use of lightning and color. The design should also take into account the restaurant's brand and the overall customer experience.

Implementation: The implementation of the restaurant's philosophy, strategy, and design is critical to its success. This includes proper staffing, menu development, and the execution of daily operations. A well-implemented plan will ensure that the restaurant is able to consistently deliver a high level of service and quality to its customers.

In summary, a good restaurant should have a clear and concise philosophy, a well-thought-out strategy, an appealing design, and a solid implementation plan. When these elements are in place, the restaurant will be well-positioned for success and able to provide a memorable dining experience for the customers.

What types of restaurants promise the most success?

There is no one type of restaurant that promises the most success in the restaurant industry depends on many factors, including the location, target market, competition, menu offerings, and overall operational execution. However, there are certain types of restaurants that have been consistently popular and profitable:

1. Fast Casual Restaurants: Fast casual restaurants offer high-quality,
   healthy food at an affordable price, in a quick and convenient format.
   This type of restaurant has been growing in popularity in recent years
   and has been successful in many markets.

2. Specialty Restaurants: Restaurants that focus on a specific type of
   cuisine or ingredient, such as sushi or seafood, can be successful if they
   offer high-quality products and a unique dining experience.

3. Fine Dining Restaurants: Fine dining restaurants can be successful if

they offer an exceptional dining experience, with a high level of service

and a menu featuring high-end ingredients. This type of restaurant

typically targets a more affluent clientele.

4. Brunch Restaurants: Brunch has become increasingly popular in

recent years, and restaurants that offer a unique brunch menu and

atmosphere can be successful.

5. Ethnic Restaurants: Ethnic restaurants that offer authentic and high-

quality cuisine from a specific culture can be successful if there is

demand for that type of food in the local market.

Ultimately, the type of restaurant that is most likely to succeed depends on the local market, competition, and the owner's ability to execute a well-defined business plan. It is important for a restaurant to understand its target market, have a clear brand identity, and offer high-quality products and service to be successful.

Of course, we could still have AI prepare a detailed business plan now if we provided the individual prompts for it. But this is just an example of how we can achieve better results with our projects in the future with the help of AI. Of course, in all areas we can imagine.

THEORIES OF THOUGHT AND PSYCHOLOGY

In the field of psychology, several theories of thought are considered to be particularly important for understanding how people form and change their opinions, beliefs, and attitudes. Some of the most influential theories include:

1. Social Cognitive Theory: The theory focuses on the role of

social and
   cultural factors in shaping beliefs and attitudes, and

emphasizes the
   importance of observing and imitating the behavior of others.

2. Social Identity Theory: This theory proposes that people's

sense of
   self is closely tied to their social identity and that they form

opinions
   and attitudes based on the beliefs and attitudes of the groups

they
   belong to.

3. Cognitive Dissonance Theory: This theory suggests that people

experience psychological discomfort when their attitudes and

behavior

are incongruent, and that they are motivated to reduce this

discomfort

by changing their attitudes or beliefs.

4. Systematic Desensitization: This therapeutic technique is

based on

classical conditioning and aims to change unwanted behavior

or

attitudes by gradually exposing the person to stimuli that

trigger those

behavior and attitudes.

5. Social Influence Theory: This theory proposes that people are
influenced by the opinions and beliefs of others, and that they

are more

likely to change their opinions in response to persuasive

messages and

social pressure.

These theories provide a framework for understanding how
people form and change their opinions and beliefs, and they
have important implications for fields such as psychology,
education, marketing, and politics. They are also subject
to ongoing research and refinement, as new findings and
insights are continually emerging in these fields.

WHAT NEW INSIGHTS ARE THERE IN CONNECTION WITH AI IN PSYCHOLOGY AND SOCIOLOGY?

The integration of Artificial Intelligence (AI) into the fields of psychology and sociology is a rapid growing area of research, and new insights are emerging all the time. Some of existing developments include:

1. Predictive models: AI algorithms are being used to develop predictive
  models that can forecast human behavior, such as the likelihood of
  someone developing a mental health condition, or their likelihood of
  engaging in criminal behavior.

2. Natural language processing: AI algorithms are being used to
  analyze large volumes of text data, such as social media posts and
  online reviews, to gain insight into public opinion and social trends.

3. Personal interventions: AI algorithms are being used to develop

personal interventions for mental health and well-being, such as

chatbots that can provide emotional support and self-help strategies.

4. Computational social science: AI algorithms are being used to

analyze large datasets and simulate human behavior, providing new

insights into social dynamics and group behavior.

5. Bias and fairness: AI algorithms have the potential to perpetuate and

amplify existing biases, and researchers are working to develop

methods for detecting and mitigating algorithmic bias in AI systems.

These developments are providing new insights into human behavior and social dynamics, and they have important implications for fields such as mental health, criminal justice, marketing, and public policy. However, it's important to acknowledge that AI is not a panacea, and that there are also challenges and ethical concerns associated with its integration into these fields, such as the potential for bias and discrimination. Ongoing research and public discussion will be crucial in ensuring that AI is used in responsible and ethical ways that benefit society as a whole.

How far will AI change learning?

Artificial intelligence (AI) has the potential to significantly change the way we approach learning. Here are some ways AI is already having an impact and how it might change learning in the future:

1. Personalized learning: AI algorithms can analyze a student's

learning
patterns and preferences, and use this information to create
customized lesson plans and educational experiences.

2. Intelligent tutoring systems: AI tutors can provide personalized
feedback, identify areas where students are struggling, and offer
targeted lessons and exercises to help them improve.

3. Automated grading and assessment: AI can be used to grade
assignments and provide feedback, freeing up teachers to focus on
other tasks.

4. Predictive analytics: AI can analyze student data to predict future
performance and identify at-risk students early on, allowing teachers to
provide targeted support.

5. Virtual reality and simulation-based learning: AI can be used to
create immersive virtual experiences that simulate real-world
scenarios, allowing students to learn in a safe, controlled environment.

In the future, AI has the potential to revolutionize education by allowing students to learn at their own pace, from anywhere, and with tailored support. However, it's important to note that AI is not a replacement for human teachers, but rather a tool that can enhance the learning experience. The role of human teachers will remain crucial in fostering critical thinking, creativity, and empathy, among other important skills.

To what extend should educators prepare for the challenge of AI?

Educators should be proactive in preparing for the challenge of

AI in education. Here are a few ways educators can prepare for the integration of AI in their teaching:

1. Stay informed about AI advancements: Educators should stay up to
date on the latest developments and innovations in AI and their
potential applications in education. They can attend conferences,
participate in professional development opportunities, and follow
relevant websites, blogs, and journals.

2. Acquire digital skills: Educators should develop their digital skills so
that they can effectively integrate technology and AI into their
teaching. They can attend workshops, online courses, or earn a digital
certification.

3. Foster critical thinking: AI has the potential to automate many tasks,
but students still need to develop critical thinking skills to make sense
of information, evaluate sources, and solve problems. Educators can
incorporate activities and assignments that encourage students to
engage in critical thinking and analyses.

4. Emphasize ethics and responsible use: AI raises important ethical
and social issues, such as privacy and data protection, bias, and
accountability. Educators should incorporate discussions about these
topics into their curriculum and encourage students to think critically

about how AI is used in society.

5. Collaborate with technology experts: Educators should collaborate
with technology experts, such as instructional designers, endtech
specialists, and AI researchers, to understand the potential and
limitations of AI and to integrate it into their teaching in meaningful
ways.

Overall, educators should approach AI as an opportunity to enhance their teaching and support student learning. By staying informed, acquiring digital skills, fostering critical thinking, emphasizing ethics and responsible use, and collaborating with technology experts, educators can prepare for the challenge of AI in education.

Teachers and professors discuss how to grade term papers that use AI!

Grading term papers that use AI can be a unique challenge rot teachers and professors. Here are some potential discussion points and considerations:

1. Understanding the role of AI in the paper: It is important to understand how the student used AI in their paper, whether it was for
research or analysis, or to generate content. This can help in assessing
the student's overall contribution to the paper and the level of understanding demonstrated.

2. Evaluation criteria: It may be necessary to establish new evaluation
criteria when grading term papers that use AI. For instance, some
possible criteria could be the quality of the AI system used, the

accuracy of the result generated, and the student's ability to interpret
and analyze the results.

3. Avoiding bias: Teachers and professors need to be aware of the
potential for bias in the AI systems used in the paper. They may need
to look at the data sources, the algorithms, and the models used to
ensure that they are accurate and unbiased.

4. Student understanding: It is important to assess the student's
understanding of the AI system used and how it was applied in the
paper. Teachers and professors may want to ask questions about the
system and how it was used to generate the results presented in the
paper.

5. Encouraging critical thinking: Teachers and professors can
encourage critical thinking by asking students to evaluate the
limitations of the AI system used and to consider alternative methods
for analyzing or generating the data.

Overall, grading term papers that use AI requires a nuanced approach, and teachers and professors need to be open to new evaluation criteria and methods. By engaging in thoughtful discussion and exploration, educators can ensure that they are fairly assessing student work and encouraging critical thinking around the use of AI in research and analysis.

To be honest, I find the expectation that teachers and professors would be able to rate all AI systems a bit naïve. I think we will have to come to a different system of grading term papers and dissertations. Perhaps it will even make sense to allow unrestricted use of AI everywhere, and those who are good at using it will have advantages.

In any case, liberalization would have the great advantage that the flow of knowledge would not be restricted. It won't be able to stop it anyway, so open access would probably bring more progress in any situation than attempts to control it.

THE SOCIOLOGY
OF PLACES

When I developed this new theory about the sociology of places back in 1982, I could not have imagined that it would play an important role in connection with artificial intelligence (AI) in 2023. What sociology is, is well known: the study of the formed transformations of human coexistence. What places are, is also generally known, however, is here not only about life on places, but especially with places. Even if it has perhaps not yet been brought to consciousness, it cannot be overlooked that people basically need a place everywhere they are and surprisingly, the best places are usually occupied.

It should be clear to everyone that the fewer places there are, the more needed places there are not. Non-existent places create conflicts! About 10 billion people on earth will want to find their place where they can not only survive but have the best life from their point of view. There are very many different types of places, and each of us, if we are mobile, has several places that we occupy during the day. The status can be different in each of the different places, which depends on different factors and roles that we can take.

The problem becomes clear if you take just one irritant word like workplace. Jobs are demanded, lost, created, destroyed, made available, sought, found, given up, defended, loved, hated. No wonder when employees write on their banners during company bankruptcies: "We want our jobs back!" When we are ousted from our place, we experience this process as a most unpleasant act. For our jobs we are ready to fight!

What happened?

Well, it's not just computers and robots, it's not just the internet that's come along, with its search engines and apps, since late 22 early 23 there's now AI for everyone. And the question we have to ask ourselves is, of course, what impact does this development have on the places we thought we had already conquered? Not just on our workplaces alone, where the change will be huge anyway, but on all the places where we have more or less settled comfortably.

Maybe I should ask AI itself what it means for jobs when everyone can suddenly do something they couldn't do before. Yes, that's a pretty good idea!

What does it mean for jobs when everyone can suddenly more with AI than before?

The increasing capabilities of AI and automation are leading to some job displacement, particularly in certain industries. However, they also have the potential to create new job opportunities and increase productivity, leading to overall economic growth.

While certain tasks previously performed by humans are being taken over by machines, the development and deployment of AI and automation technologies is also creating new job roles in fields such as data science, machine learning engineering, and software development. Additionally, as automation becomes more widespread, there will likely be a growing demand for people with skills in areas such as project management, process design, and change management, as well as those who can work with AI systems and interpret their outputs.

It's important to note that while AI has the potential to make certain jobs obsolete, it can also augment human skills and make many jobs more efficient and effective. Rather than replacing human workers entirely, AI is likely to change the tasks they perform and the way they perform them, and it will be up to both individuals and society as a whole to adapt and thrive in this new landscape.

There are not only jobs, people occupy other places in society!

Yes, that's correct. People occupy many different roles and positions in society, not just in the workforce. The impact of AI on society goes beyond just employment and job displacement. It also has the potential to affect many aspects of daily life, including education, healthcare, transportation, and communication.

For example, AI can be used to improve educational outcomes by personalizing learning experience, providing real-time feedback, an enabling the creation of immersive virtual environments. In healthcare, AI can be used to diagnose diseases more accurately, developed personalized treatment plans, and improve patient outcomes. In transportation, AI can be used to optimize routes, reduce traffic congestion, and improve safety. And in communication, Ai can be used to enhance natural language processing, provide personalized recommendations, and improve overall experience.

While AI has the potential to bring about many positive changes in these areas, it also raises important ethical and social questions about privacy, fairness, and the distribution of benefits. It's important for society to consider these questions and ensure that the development and deployment of AI is aligned with our values and priorities.

In detail, how can AI be prevented from increasing inequality in the world?

Preventing AI from increasing inequality in the world requires a multi-faceted approach that considers the ethical, social, and economic implications of AI, and takes proactive steps to ensure that its benefits are distributed fairly and equitably. Here are a few strategies that can help:

1. Invest in education and upskilling: To ensure that everyone has the
opportunity to participate in the AI-driven economy, it's important to
invest in education and upskilling programs that help people acquire
the skills they need to succeed in the new job market. This includes not
only technical skills in areas such as data science and machine learning,
but also skills such as critical thinking, problem-solving, and collaboration.

2. Address bias in AI systems: AI systems are only as fair and
unbiased as the data and algorithms used to build them. It's important
to identify and address sources of bias in AI systems, and to develop
and implement strategies to mitigate them. This includes efforts to
collect more diverse and representative data, and to test AI systems for
fairness and bias before they are deployed.

3. Foster inclusive AI ecosystems: To ensure that AI benefits
everyone, it's important to create inclusive AI ecosystems that promote
collaboration and partnership between different stakeholders, including
government, academia, the private sector, and civil society. This can
help to ensure that the needs and perspectives of marginalized
communities are considered and addressed in the development and

deployment of AI.

4. Regulate AI development and use: Effective regulation can help to
ensure that AI is developed and used in ways that promote fairness,
transparency, and accountability. This includes efforts to establish clear
guidelines for the ethical use of AI, and hold companies and governments accountable for the impact of their AI systems on individuals and communities.

5. Promote economic growth and inclusion: To ensure that the benefits of AI are widely distributed, it's important to promote economic growth and inclusion. This includes efforts to reduce poverty
and inequality, create good jobs, and provide access to essential services such as health care, education, and transportation.

These are just a few of the strategies that can help prevent AI from increasing inequality in the world. Addressing these challenges will require a coordinated effort from all sectors of society, and will require us to be proactive and creative in our approaches.

We have 64 percent internet users worldwide in 2023, but one third has still no access!

Despite the rapid growth of the internet and the many benefits it provides, there are still significant disparities in access to digital technologies, including the internet.

This digital divide has significant implications for economic, social, and political development, as access to the internet is increasingly becoming a prerequisite for participation in the global economy, education, and political discourse. The lack of access to the internet also exacerbates existing inequalities, as those who are already disadvantaged are often the ones who are least likely to have access to digital technologies.

To address this issue, there is a growing movement to promote digital inclusion and ensure that everyone has access to the internet and the opportunities it provides. This includes efforts to expand the infrastructure and increase access to affordable devices and internet services, as well as programs to develop digital literacy and provide training and support for those who need it. Additionally, policies and regulations that promote net neutrality and protect the rights of internet users can help ensure that the internet users can help ensure that the internet remains a space for free expression and innovation.

Closing the digital divide is an important goal that requires the cooperation of governments, businesses, civil society, and individuals. Ny working together, we can help ensure that everyone has the opportunity to participate in the digital world and reap its benefits.

Thesis: The more unequal the places, the greater the potential for conflict!

How is it in love?

Our desire is always to conquer a very specific place, for example, a place in the heart of another person. Although, of course, we know that this is completely irrational because the heart is actually a hollow muscle, and the place we want to reach is in the brain. Anyway, the brain is less romantic because it is not heart-shaped, does not throb and ache, but visually resembles half of a walnut kernel.

In order to attain this eagerly hoped-for place in the heart of our beloved, we sometimes have to put up quite a bit. We have to come up with something without jumping right in. Now, this complicates the matter, in the human heart there are sometimes numerous places to be given and often non at all. It is by no means the case that two people who want to reach places in each other's hearts always assign pale-sized places to each other.

It also often happens that people have reserved a place in their heart for someone who no longer has one free and often do not know about it. In the age of mass communication, this one-sided reservation of space, the star cult, has reached quite thought-blocking dimensions. Added to this are the dating platforms, on which millions of people cavort who look and think differently than they pretend. So far, it doesn't really seem to have been proven that getting to know someone through the new possibilities would definitely have made things easier. The question is therefore justified as to how far AI will begiven a field of activity here.

How can AI improve dating?

AI con improve dating in several ways, including:

1. Personalized matchmaking: AI algorithms can analyze vast amounts
   of data users' preferences, behavior, and personality to offer more
   accurate and personalized matchmaking.

2. Fraud detection: AI can help identify and prevent fraud by analyzing
   user behavior patterns and detecting fake profiles.

3. Chatbots: AI-powered chatbots can help users engage in more
   meaningful conversations and improve their communication skills.

4. Image recognition: AI can analyze profile pictures to detect fake to
   or inappropriate images, and ensure that user's photos are
   representative of their actual appearance.

5. Feedback and recommendations: AI can provide feedback and recommendations to users on how to improve their profiles, communication skills, and dating experiences.

Are there studies about dating experiences?

Yes, there are many studies about dating experiences. Researchers have explored various aspects of dating, such as:

1. Online dating: Studies have examined how people use online dating
   platforms, their motivations for using them, and how online dating
   compares to traditional dating.

2. Attraction and mate selection: Research has explored the factors
   that contribute to attraction and mate selection, such as physical
   attractiveness, personality, and shared interests.

3. Communication and interaction: Studies have investigated how
   people communicate and interact on dates, including how they initiate
   and maintain conversations, the role of nonverbal cues, and the impact
   of technology on communication.

4. Dating and mental health: Research has explored the relationship
   between dating experiences and mental health outcomes, such as
   anxiety, depression, and self-esteem.

Overall, the study of dating experiences is a rich and diverse field of research that has important implications for our understanding of human relationship and well-being.

How will AI change dating in the future?

AI is expected to have a significant impact on the future dating. Here're some potential ways AI could change dating:

1. More accurate matchmaking: AI algorithms will become more
    sophisticated, allowing or even more accurate and personalized
   matchmaking. This could help people find better matches and potentially lead to more successful relationships.

2. Improved safety and security: AI-powered fraud detection and
    image recognition technology could help ensure that dating platforms
   are safe and secure, reducing the risk of scams, catfishing, and other
   forms of online dating fraud.

3. Enhanced communication: AI-powered chatbots and natural
    language processing could help improve communication between users,
   making it easier to initiate and maintain conversation.

4. Virtual dating experiences: As virtual and augmented reality
    technology improves, AI could help create more realistic and engaging
   virtual dating experiences, allowing people to connect with potential
   partners in more immersive ways.

5. More personalized feedback and coaching: As AI becomes better
    at analyzing user behavior and preferences, it could provide more
   personalized feedback and coaching to help people improve their dating
   skills and find more compatible matches.

Overall, AI is expected to play an increasingly important role in the future of dating, potentially making it easier, safer, and more successful for people to find romantic partners.

What role will AI play in dating avatars in the Metaverse?

As the Metaverse continue to develop, AI is likely to play a significant role in creating and enhancing dating avatars. Here are some potential ways AI could be used in dating avatars:

1. Avatar customization: AI algorithms could analyze user data, preferences, and behavior to help create highly personalized avatars
that accurately reflect users' identities and preferences.

2. Emotional expression: AI could help avatars express a wider range of
emotions and respond to users' emotional cues, creating a more
immersive and engaging dating experience.

3. Realistic interaction: AI-powered natural language processing and
speech recognition could help avatars interact with users in a more
realistic and natural way, making conversations feel more like those in
real life.

4. Relationship coaching: AI could analyze users' interactions with their
avatars and provide personalized feedback and coaching to help them
improve their communication and relationship skills.

5. Safety and security: AI-powered fraud detection and image recognition technology could help ensure that avatars are save and secure, reducing the risks of scams, catfishing, and other forms of

online dating fraud.

Overall, AI is likely to play a crucial role in creating engaging and effective dating avatars in the Metaverse, potentially making it easier and more enjoyable for people to find romantic partners in virtual environments.

Two avatars meet in the Metaverse: one whispers, we'll go to you or to me? The other says softly, to me, but don't tell anyone else!

What I mean by that, it all still sounds a bit like the brave new world. I do believe that that AI con be useful in many professions and also in private life, if self-thinking is not neglected, because writing and speaking are already reduced today.

What is love from a scientific point of view?

We are in the realm of neurobiology and psychology when we research love. It is quite astonishing that man, of all people, strives for a longer bond in his partnership, while only a few mammals do the same. There is a theory for this because our brain has grown so much through evolution and the head has become so large that human children have to be born immature because they cannot pass through the birth canal.

The pregnant and birthing women could no longer provide food on their own, and at least some of the fathers were willing to participate in the search for edibles, establishing this genetic variant over time. In this way, they ensured the survival of their offspring, while the survival chances of the children of fathers who did not form a close bond with the mother of their children were reduced. Nature did not design us to stay together forever, but it is a cultural idea of what an ideal relationship should be like.

It cannot be assumed that soul mates actually exist, but there is a strict neurochemical roadmap for infatuation. The level of the neurotransmitter dopamine and the stress hormone cortisol increase, while the neurotransmitter serotonin decreases. This activates our reward system in the brain, but this only lasts for a few months and up to a year. Time enough in the sense of evolution to conceive a child and then, after the state of infatuation, to reach the phase of love or to separate.

We don't really know beforehand whether we can actually form a long-term bond with the partner we fall in love with and have children with. In this respect, it is also by no means certain that similar interests automatically lead to marriages or partnerships that are happy for a long time.

How do infatuation and love come about?

Infatuation is a strong attraction or admiration for someone that is typically short-lived and based on external qualities. Love, on the other hand, is a deeper emotional connection that develops over time and is based on a combination of physical, emotional, and intellectual compatibility. Infatuation can be sparked by physical appearance or a brief encounter, while love usually requires getting to know someone on a more intimate level and building a connection through shared experiences and mutual respect. Hormones such as dopamine and serotonin are involved in both infatuation and love, but the difference lies in the depth and duration of emotional attachment.

Why then do about a third of all partnerships fail?

There are many reasons why about a third of all partnerships fail, and the specific reasons can vary from one couple to another. Some common reasons for relationship breakdowns include:

1. Communication problems: This can include poor communication,
   misunderstandings, or a lack of communication altogether.

2. Incompatibility: Differences in personality, values, and life

goals can
create tension in a relationship over time.

3. Infidelity: Cheating or other forms of betrayal can break down trust
and lead to the end of a relationship.

4. Money issues: Financial stress or disagreement over spending can
create tension and conflict in a relationship.

5. Life changes: Major life events such a job loss, illness, or a birth of a
child can put strain on a relationship.

6. Lack of effort: A relationship requires effort and attention from both
partners to thrive, and neglect or complacency can lead to its downfall.

Ultimately, every relationship is unique, and the reason for its success or failure can be complex and multifaceted.

How can AI help save a partnership?

While AI is not a substitute for human connection and understanding, it can assist in various ways to help save a partnership. Here are some potential ways AI can help:

1. Relationship counseling: AI-powered chatbots can offer virtual
counseling sessions and provide helpful advice to couples experiencing
communication problems or conflicts.

2. Emotional monitoring: AI can monitor a couple's communication
patterns, voice tones, and other emotional signals to provide insights
into their emotional state and help detect potential conflicts

before they
    escalate.

3. Personalized recommendations: AI algorithms can analyze a
    couple's communication and behavior patterns to offer
personalized
    recommendations for ways to improve their relationship, such
as
    suggesting activities they can do together or strategies for
better
    communication.

4. Virtual support groups: AI-powered virtual support groups
can offer
    couples a safe space to discuss their challenges with other
couples and
    receive support and advice from experts.

While AI can be a helpful tool, it is important to remember
that human connection and understanding are essential
for the success of any partnership. AI should not replace
human communication, empathy, and compassion, but rather
complement it.

The topic of narcissism in relationships is a hot topic in the
media right now. Hence the question:

**How can male and female narcissist disrupt their
relationships?**

Both male and female narcissists can disrupt their relationships
in similar ways. Narcissists tend to have an exaggerated sense of
self-importance and entitlement, a lack of empathy, and a need
for constant admiration and attention.

In relationship, a narcissist may constantly seek validation and
attention from their partner, while also belittling and devaluing
them. They may be prone to emotional outbursts and have a
tendency to manipulate their partner in order to remain control

over the relationship.

Male and female narcissists may disrupt their relationships by engaging in behaviors such as gaslighting, love bombing, and emotional abuse. They may also have a tendency to cheat and engage in other forms of infidelity.

Overall, a relationship with a narcissist can be very difficult and challenging, and it is important for both partners to seek professional help if they are struggling to maintain a healthy and happy relationship.

Thesis: Prominence creates places, but also requires some!

When a celebrity walks into a fancy restaurant, what happens? Exactly, the table is usually vacated in the best position. Of course, it cannot be overlooked that celebrities are also dependent on always getting the best seats because otherwise their image as a celebrity suffers. There's no question that being in the media all the time can be stressful, but my sympathy is limited.

Thesis: If you don't have a suitable place, you become neglected and get sick!

If you are homeless or do not keep the place where you live in order, you are sick. In alcoholics and drug addicts, this environmental symptom is usually evident. It is also true when parents neglect their children or when pet owners neglect their animals. A mental illness is always to blame.
The existence and condition of the place one inhabits is of extremely great importance for our well-being.

Question: To what extent can AI improve the living situation?

AI has the potential to significantly improve the living situation in various ways, such as enhancing healthcare, optimizing energy consumption, improving transportation, and increasing efficiency in various industries. However, the extent to which

AI can improve the living situation ultimately depends on the responsible and ethical development, and use of AI systems by individuals and organizations. AI should be developed and utilized in a way that respects human rights, privacy, and safety and benefits society as a whole.

It has been shown that at the present time AI cannot make clear statements about the improvements in the quality of life and the participation of people who are threatened by poverty and have no access to modern technology. I do expect that there will be a lot of movement here in the coming years, also because of the rapidly developing race in the AI sector between the big players in 2023.

FEW PLACES, MANY APPLICANTS

At the top of the pyramid, when we look at corporate hierarchies, the air gets very thin. The same applies to all institutions. Few make it up there. More people, if not all, want to get to the top. These particularly coveted positions are known to be extremely scarce. Reaching one of these places in the sun is a goal recognized as sensible by the majority in all forms of society. Why shouldn't that be our goal?

There is an unmanageable amount of literature that deals with how to survive in the management jungle. But all this advice is only applicable to a limited extent, because there are too many of them and some contradict each other. The easiest way to do nothing wrong is to do nothing at all. One should be polite and friendly, but at the same time assertive. Sincere and refined, cool and cordial, ambitious and modest.

Instead, I would like to put forward a number of further theses to stimulate new thinking:

Economics is exclusively about places!

It's the same when we talk about companies, it's about what rank they have in the industry, what location is the best, what trade show spaces, shelf spaces, ad spaces are the best. With people we talk about their places inside the company, and outside about building places and market places. For multinationals, we are even talking about the places they can gain, hold and improve worldwide. Those who have understood in good time that the entire economic effort is essentially about places can adjust accordingly and fill the vacant place as quickly as possible before the competition does.

Of course, the question immediately arises as to how AI can help to put this knowledge into practice in a particularly beneficial way. Let's just ask our favorite chatbot!

How can AI support the race to the top in business?

AI can support the race to the top in business by providing advanced data analytics and automation capabilities that can optimize processes and decision-making. AI can help businesses better understand customers behavior, identify new opportunities, and streamline operations for improved efficiency and cost savings. AI can also facilitate the development of new products and services, and enhance customer experience through personalized interactions and predictive insights.

Would you agree with the thesis that economics strive to win places?

As an AI language model, I do not have personal opinions or belief, but to the best of my knowledge, the thesis that economics strives to win places does not accurately represent the field of economics. Economics is a social science that seeks to understand how individuals, businesses, and governments allocate scarce resources to satisfy unlimited wants and needs. It is concerned with the production, consumption, and distribution of goods and services, and how economic actors interact within markets and institutions. While economic activity may involve competition for resources and market share, the ultimate goal of economics is to improve the welfare and standard of living of individuals and society as a whole, rather than simply "winning places".

What about the rankings, the fight for market share and shelf

space, as well as for management positions?

It is true that rankings, market share, shelf space, and management positions are all relevant factors in business competition. However, while economics is concerned with the study of markets and competition, its goal is not simply to "win places" but to understand how markets work and how resources can be allocated efficiently to benefit society as a whole.

In a market economy, businesses compete for customers, market share, and profits. This competition can be beneficial to consumers by promoting innovation, reducing prices, and improving product quality. However, the goal of economics is not to promote competition for its own sake, but to understand how markets work and to develop policies that promoting efficiency and welfare.

Furthermore, economics is a broad and interdisciplinary field that encompasses many different topics, including macroeconomic policy, international trade, behavioral economics, and development economics. While market competition is an important part of the economic landscape, it is not the only focus of the discipline, and economists study a wide range of economic phenomena beyond just market competition.

From the chatbot's answers it becomes clear that it cannot grasp the pointing to a somewhat provocative term, bat basically describes the market economy as conservative economists like to see it. Although critical thinking is possible, innovative thinking is not the discipline that one can currently expect. Still, what we can learn from the answer is that we can get inspiration and a broader perspective, which can definitely be a positive thing.

In terms of the sociology of places, we distinguish between people who take their own places and those who are forced to let themselves be assigned. It's a question of self-confidence. For it cannot be taken for granted that the places assigned are better than those one wanted. In democracies, this state of inequality can probably be overcome through personal effort, but in totalitarian states with surveillance systems, rebellion against injustice is less possible. Therefore, AI must be prevented from being used to perfect surveillance.

THE ART OF BECOMING AN ARTIST

Michelangelo said: "The art that follows the intellect can accomplish achievements. And Picasso said: "There are painters who turn the sun into a yellow spot. But there are others who, thank their art and intelligence, can turn a yellow spot into the sun." Two of the greatest artists this world has ever seen very clearly associate art with the mind. Art doesn't happen by accident.

In the meantime, everyone who deals with artificial intelligence knows that AI can not only write texts, but can also generate images based on prompts. Namely pictures of fairly good quality and amazing imagination. The question that immediately arises: Will AI eclipse all visual artists in the future? Will painters, designers, graphic artists become unemployed and redundant? What is happening in this art sector? Maybe our machine friend can provide the answer for that!

What will happen to the visual arts in the future if AI develops further?

It is difficult to predict the exact impact that AI will have on the visual arts in the future, as it will depend on a variety of factors, such as the development of AI technology, the ways in which artists choose to incorporate AI into their creative process, and the preferences of audiences and the art market. However, it is likely that AI will continue to play a growing role in the creation and interpretation of visual art, potentially leading to new forms of expression and aesthetic experiences. At the same time, it may also raise questions about authorship, creativity, and the role of human artists in the creative process.

The speed at which AI is already creating works of art is beyond the power of a performing artist!

It is true that AI can generate works of art at an unprecedented speed, but it is important to note that AI-generated art is fundamentally different from art created by human performers. While AI may be able to generate art quickly and efficiently, it lacks the emotional depth, subjectivity, and improvisational qualities that are often associated with human artistic expression. Moreover, many people value art not just for its aesthetic qualities, but also for the cultural and historical contexts, social commentary, and personal connections that it embodies. While AI-generated art may be impressive in its own right, it is unlikely to replace the rich and diverse tapestry of human artistic expression.

Contemporary art and works by famous artists can already be transformed into new works in their style with AI! It's happening now, early 2023, I've seen it with my own eyes. Certainly, some things are not yet mature, but it is conceivable that this is exactly what will happen like an avalanche. From my point of view, I'm not only an author, but also a painter and designer, this is a development that can lead to enormous problems. Not so much for myself, but for all those who want to make a living from their art.

Another Chatbot answers: The rise of AI-generated art has raised some interesting questions about the future of the art world. For one, it has become much easier for anyone to create art that looks like it was created by a famous artist, potentially taking away from the value of the original artwork. Additionally, this could lead to copyright issues as AI-generated art could potentially resemble the style of an artist without their permission.

On the other hand, AI-generated art could also provide new opportunities for artists, as it could be used to produce artworks quickly and efficiently, or to generate new and unique art that would otherwise be difficult or impossible to create. It could also help to expand the art market, as AI-generated art could be a more affordable alternative to traditional artworks. Ultimately, the impact of AI-generated art on the art world is still uncertain, but it is certainly an exciting development.

The only question is, for whom?

At the beginning of every truly significant work of art is new and unusual thinking. For a painting, a sculpture, a play, a novel of world literature – always and in every case, it is a defamiliarization of reality. Art is never the faithful reflection of reality, but either more, i.e. dramatization, or less, i.e. reduction. Great art generally uses these two options sparingly. It ideally finds the right measure – and this is now a difficult intellectual task, because there are infinitely more chances to miss this right measure than to hit it.

There is a threefold difficulty that the artist has to overcome when first wants to create art:

1. a problem of craftsmanship
2. a creative problem
3. an independent style

The secret to practicing art is trial and error and practice. It is not necessary to be gifted. Anyone can accomplish artistic feats that are satisfying to oneself. That alone is what matters. The professional artist also had manual difficulties at the beginning, which he did not let deter him from finding his way.

The artist, who can stamp a personal style for his creation, makes a unique achievement. Who wants to decide whether this work is good or bad? Especially not moral judgments should be made, because artistic performance is neutral in this regard. In art, everything that does not violate laws is allowed. Unwritten design laws may be violated anyway. Atonal music, graffiti painting, protest songs, nonsense texts, Dadaism are certainly not everyone's cup of tea. Ranked art has its raison d'etre because it raises awareness.

If art is allowed to do almost anything, there is one thing it must not do: bore! Maybe I should ask chatbot what it thinks!

What is art allowed and what is not?

Art is allowed to express ideas and thoughts, as long as it does not violate legal and ethical standards. It is important to remember that art can be interpreted in different ways, so it is important to consider the potential impact of your artwork before publishing it. Generally speaking, art should not contain any offensive, hateful, defamatory, or obscene material. Additionally, it should not contain any copyrighted material unless permission has been granted by the copyright holder.

Are the texts of a chatbot subject to copyright?

Generally speaking, the texts generated by a chatbot are not subject to copyright protection. This is because the texts generated by a chatbot are not created by a human author, but rather by a machine. However, in some cases, the texts by a chatbot may contain components that are subject to copyright protection, such as quotes or text taken from other sources. In these cases, the copyright status of the text will depend on the source of the material.

In the texts of the chatbots there are no references, how should one pay attention to them? To the best of my knowledge this question has not yet been resolved. In any case, at the time I saw chatbot texts, I did not see any links to sources and authors. Which doesn't have to be surprising, because the texts are written by a machine that evaluates a huge amount of data.

Why is analog painting becoming important alongside digital possibilities?

It is not only passive art viewing and admiration for masterpieces, but everyone can be an artist. Not always in the so-called bread and butter profession, but in their free time. Anyone can paint, pottery, emailing, carving, embroidery and work and shape all these wonderful materials that nature has given us.

While in reading signs must be deciphered in their meaning, which is not possible for everyone, because on our earth several thousand languages and dialects as well as illiteracy and ignorance are widespread, painting is suitable to convey an experience. Art does not have to be interpreted. It can have an immediate effect on our feelings.

Thesis: Thinking connects art and nature.

It is something completely natural to create art. Just as it is artificial to want to create nature. This brings us directly to the subject of natural and artificial intelligence.

What is the difference between artificial and natural intelligence?

Artificial intelligence (AI) and natural intelligence (NI) are two fundamentally different types of intelligence.
Natural intelligence refers to the intelligence that is possessed by living beings such as humans, animals, and even some plants. This type of intelligence is the product of millions of years of evolution and enables us to solve problems, reason, understand language, learn, and adapt to new situations.

Artificial intelligence, on the other hand, refers to the intelligence exhibited by machines that are programmed to perform cognitive tasks that would typically require human intelligence. AI involves the development of computer algorithms and systems that can perform tasks that normally require human intelligence, such as understanding natural language, recognizing patterns, and making decisions.

While natural intelligence is highly flexible and adaptive, artificial intelligence is designed to perform specific tasks efficiently and accurately. However, AI lacks the versatility and creativity of natural intelligence and cannot match the flexibility and adaptability of human beings.

In summary, natural intelligence is the product of evolution and is possessed by living beings, while artificial intelligence is the result of human-created technology that enables machines to perform tasks that would normally require human intelligence.

AI and NI Collaboration

In which fields can AI and NI best be combined?

AI (Artificial Intelligence) and NI (Natural Intelligence) can be combined in various fields to achieve more effective and efficient outcomes. Here are a few examples of fields where AI and NI can best be combined:

1. Healthcare: AI and NI can be used together to improve patient care,
diagnosis, and treatment. For example, AI algorithms can analyze
medical data and images, while doctors and nurses can use their
natural intelligence to interpret the results and make informed decisions.

2. Education: AI can be used to personalize learning experiences based
on student's individual needs and abilities, while teachers can use their
natural intelligence to provide support and guidance to students.

3. Finance: AI can be used to analyze large amounts of financial data and
  make predictions, while financial experts can use their natural
    intelligence to make informed decisions based on their experience and
  expertise.

4. Manufacturing: AI can be used to optimize production processes and
  improve efficiency, while human workers can use their natural
    intelligence to oversee and manage the manufacturing process.

5. Transportation: AI can be used to optimize transportation routes and
  reduce fuel consumption, while human drivers and pilots can use their
    natural intelligence to make decisions and take action in unexpected
  situations.

6. Entertainment: AI can be used to personalize recommendations for
    movies, TV shows, and music, while human critics and reviewers can
  use their natural intelligence to provide in-depth analysis and
  commentary.

Overall, the combination of AI and NI can lead to more accurate and efficient outcomes in various fields, while also leveraging the strengths of both human and machine intelligence.

What connections can Artists for their work with AI and NI make?

Artists can use AI (Artificial Intelligence) and NI (Natural Intelligence) in many different ways to create new forms of artistic expression and explore new possibilities in their work.

One example of this is the use of generative adversarial networks (GANs) in art. GANs are a type of AI algorithm that can generate new images or other media based on patterns in existing data. By training a GAN on a large dataset of images or other media, an artist can create a tool that generates new, unique artworks that reflect the characteristics of the training data. The artists can then use their natural intelligence to curate and refine the results, selecting the most interesting and compelling works for exhibition or further development.

Another example is the use of AI to analyze and interpret existing works of art. For example, AI algorithms can be used to analyze the visual features of a painting or sculpture, or to identify patterns in the use of color or composition. This analysis can help the artist gain new insights into their own work, or to create new works that explore the themes or styles of other artists in new ways.

Finally, artists can also use AI and NI together to create interactive work of art that respond to the viewer in real-time. By using sensors or other input devices to detect the viewer's movements or actions, an artist can create a work that evolves and changes over time, in response to the viewer's engagement with it.

Overall, the connection between AI and NI in art offer many exiting possibilities for artists to explore new forms of expression and to create works that reflect the complex interplay between human and machine intelligence.

INFO GAPS AND AI

In 1984 – note the year – I could not yet know that in 2023, almost 40 years later, I would have to explain a connection between my information theory and artificial intelligence. But that's exactly what happened and I am quite happy to be able to derive important insights from it.

Claims made with exclusivity always seem provocative, especially when I represent the following:

ALL OUR PROBLEMS
ARE ULTIMATELY
DUE TO

MISSING OR INADEQUATE INFORMATION!

Immediately, of course, one can question whether it can really be that literally all of mankind's problems can be traced back to the fact that we lack sufficient information.

Superficially, one may come to different opinions, which is mainly explained by the fact that there are things between heaven and earth that cannot be explained. We actually don't know very much, nevertheless there are information processes in connection with this unsatisfactory phenomenon. Consequently, it does not mean at all, if the whole science is in the dark, that there is neither one-sided information nor two-sided communication, but both are permanent events.

The entire functioning of natural life processes is based on information. If disturbances occur here, for example if the hormonal control processes fail, diseases can result. We do not even yet have the right solutions for all diagnostic possibilities, nor for all therapeutic options, because we lack the information. However, by combining natural and artificial intelligence, we can make considerable progress in this field. In any case, the chances of being able to intervene in a more personalized way on the part of physicians should increase.

We have info gaps of varying degrees in all areas, and to make matters worse, info gaps exist in controllable and uncontrollable forms. It is often difficult to distinguish the controllable gaps from the uncontrollable ones, which we can not influence. Knowing everything is as impossible as communicating with everyone. To develop complex areas of knowledge completely without gaps is impossible. In addition, the Internet and so-called social media mean that there is more and more zero information, which is of no value for the receiver, but can sometimes be significant for the sender and his status.

Today's hope is that AI will succeed in spinning a fact net in many areas. This will only succeed if AI is fed with much more correct than incorrect data and most incorrect information can be filtered out automatically. This will be a never-ending process that requires a lot of control effort. For it has become apparent that a struggle for political dominance has emerged not only between the individual major players on the world stage, but also numerous middle powers.

How does AI fill the info gaps with knowledge?

Artificial intelligence (AI) uses various techniques and approaches to fill in information gaps and acquire knowledge. Here are some ways in which AI can fill the info gaps:

1. Machine learning: Machine learning algorithms can analyze large
   amounts of data and learn patterns and trends that can be used to fill
   in missing information. For example, if there is missing data in a
      dataset, machine learning algorithms can use the available data to
   make predictions about the missing value.

2. Natural Language Processing: Natural language processing (NLP) is
      a branch of AI that deals with the interaction between computers and

human language. NLP techniques can be used to extract information

from unstructured data that can be used to fill in information gaps.

3. Knowledge Graphs: Knowledge Graphs are a type of database that

store information in a graph structure, where nodes represent entities

and edges represent the relationships between them. Knowledge

graphs can be used to connect different pieces of information and fill in

gaps by inferring new relationships between entities.

4. Data Fusion: Data fusion is the process of combining data from

multiple sources to create a more complete picture. AI can be used to

analyze and integrate data from different sources, such as social

media, new articles, and sensor data, to fill in missing information.

5. Human-in-the-Loop: In some cases, AI can work in tandem with

humans to fill in information gaps. For example, AI can be used to

generate possible solutions or answers to a problem, which can then be

reviewed and refined by a human expert.

Overall, AI can be a powerful tool for filling in information gaps and acquiring knowledge. However, it is important to note that AI is not infallible and can make errors or biases, so it is essential to carefully evaluate the results produced by AI systems.

Thesis: Info gaps can insure and unsure. It depends on how

much imagination we have.

Even filling in small gaps in information can sometimes be a problem if it is only to master mundane everyday situations. We can get distracted and, if we turn to much to something else, miss the sensible order of filling our info gaps. In theoretical considerations this is irrelevant, because it is usually a longer process. But in actions, misbehavior can lead to accidents, such as in traffic. The quoted human failure is usually due to a wrong information sequence.

Thesis: We cannot fill up very different info gaps at the same time, but only one after the other.

To be blunt, this thesis does not contradict multi-tasking. Because in this case known actions and not suddenly surprising actions are mastered. It should be said that people often have exaggerated ideas about this ability.

As early as 1984, in my book "Info gaps – Management by Information", I pointed out that the confusingly proliferating field of electronic data processing had caused large sections of the working population to fear for the future. This is still true almost 40 years later, and to a far from lesser extent. It remains to be seen whether AI will have a positive effect here. When I wrote back then that we are being driven less and less by instincts and more and more by information in our behavior, AI was still a long way off. This evolutionary process over millions of years is not yet over and we know its stage only up to the present.

With this big step into AI era, there will be a division between those people who have learned to access information and those who cannot. It is absolutely clear that the informed human being is further removed from the uninformed human being than in earlier times because he has the vehicle of technological information transfer at his disposal.

Thesis: The authoritarian ruler thinks he has nothing to learn

Wherever someone has power over others, be it individuals or entire nations, info gaps tend to have a devasting effect. There is a serious difference between a ruler misjudging the situation and just a private citizen.

Maybe the concept of artificial intelligence (AI) means something different to everyone, but the impact AI is having on society is indisputable. We have to keep in mind that every new information technology changes almost everything, but there is a key difference with AI: it uses artificial intelligence, not human intelligence.

It is not overly significant for society whether I as an author have been right with my predictions, but for me it is to some extent. It might even be interesting to quote one of my texts from 1983:

"Man does not live by knowledge alone, but it helps him to help himself. That is, to fill one's own personal info gaps. I consider nature and art – the knowledge of both – to be the most important. It is not by chance that the info gaps in these two fields, when broadly defined, are the greatest. Nevertheless, I am not an opponent of technology. This attitude may be surprising, but it can be explained by the fact that with the help of modern communication technology we will be able to close our relevant info gaps relatively easily and comprehensively in the future. For it will be the case that we will soon be able to bring all of humanity's knowledge into our living rooms. Via screen and telephone. Because we will then be able to access all essential information, provided we know what we want to know."

The most important keywords in this historical text, which I did not want to deprive you of, are in fact of extremely high relevance today:

Nature, Art, Communication, Technology, Info Gaps, Screen, Telephone -provided we know what we want to know! This is what AI is all about – we have to be able to ask the right questions!

Thesis: The content of information is more important than the form of its presentation

The statement "The content of information is more important than the form of its presentation" is a complex one and can be interpreted in different ways depending on the context. Here are a few possible interpretations and my thoughts on each:

1. Content is more important than form in terms of understanding:
In this interpretation, the statement suggests that the substance of the
information being presented is more important than the way it is
presented. In other words, as long as a message is clear and accurate,
the details of how it is communicated (e.g., in writing, speech, or a
visual format) are less important.

While the accuracy and clarity of the information are certainly
important, the form of presentation can play a significant role in how
effectively the information is conveyed and understood. For example,
certain types of information may be more effectively communicated

through visual aids, while others may be better suited to written or

spoken communication. In addition, the language and tone used to

present information can also impact its effectiveness, particularly in

situations where the information is intended to persuade or influence.

2. Content is more important than form in terms of value: In the

interpretation, the statement suggests that the intrinsic worth of the

information being presented is more important than the way it is

presented. For example, if a scientific study contains groundbreaking

findings, the value of those findings is more important than the way the

study was designed or the language used to report the results.

In general, it is true that the value of the information being presented

is an important consideration. However, the way that information is

presented can also impact its perceived value. For example, a well-

designed and visually appealing report may be perceived as more

valuable than a poorly designed report, even if the content is identical.

3. Content and form are equally important: In this interpretation, the

statement suggests that both the substance of the information being

presented and the way it is presented are equally important.

This is likely the most accurate interpretation of the statement, as both
content and form are important considerations in effective
communication. While the accuracy and value of the information are
critical, the way that information is presented can impact its reception
and effectiveness. In order to communicate effectively. It is important
to consider both the substance of the message and the way it is presented.

The leeway theory in relationships

The leeway theory in relationships is a concept that suggests that partners in a romantic relationship should give each other some degree of flexibility or "leeway" when it comes to certain behavior. This theory recognizes that individuals have their own unique personality traits, values and behavior that may differ from their partner's.

According to the leeway theory, partners should not expect their significant other to always conform to their expectations or act in a certain way. Instead, they should allow for some degree of individuality and flexibility in their relationship. For example, if one partner is more introverted and prefers to spend time alone, the other partner should respect that and not pressure them to constantly socialize.

However, the leeway theory does not mean that partners should tolerate behavior that are harmful and disrespectful. There are certain behaviors that should not be accepted in a healthy relationship, such as cheating, physical or emotional abuse, or dishonesty.

Ultimately. The leeway theory suggests that partners in a relationship should strive for a balance between individuality and mutual respect. They should be open to compromise and understanding each other's needs while still maintaining their own sense of self.

This is the text a chatbot wrote about the leeway theory in 2023!

And now comes the text I wrote in 1983 about the leeway theory. Well, it's published in one of my books, but I can't imagine the bot read it, because it's not written in English and it's not translated into that language. It probably wasn't one of my numerus theories that I put forward. But maybe it is! Such an AI can make you doubt what you not only thought at some point, but also wrote down and printed!

"The leeway theory is superior to the commonly applied bottleneck management mainly because it is easier to use existing clearances than to laboriously open bottlenecks first. In addition, you never know in advance whether a bottleneck can really be used in the intended sense. Life partners often do not leave themselves enough leeway. In particular, they do not do so when the leeway of one is significantly greater than that of the other. If there are big distances in the mental and physical area, no matter if they really exist or if they are only experienced that way. The latter, by the way, occurs incomparably more often.

Communication has a very decisive role in establishing the leeway or scope in partnerships. The more clearly it is discussed in advance, the greater the leeway that is mutually accepted. The success of a partnership does not necessarily depend on the equality of opinions and behavior. An overlapping of the margins can have a positive effect and the more tolerant someone is, the smaller this overlapping can be.

There are factors on which there should be consensus, such as where to live, how to raise children, clothing, furnishings, food, and sexuality. But when it comes to hobbies and leisure activities, leeway makes sense and is possible under understanding partners."

I think I can demonstrate that the empirical science of the lawful connections between experience and behavior, psychology, not everything has to be new in order to be still valid. But one thig is also clear from my point of view, we can review our thoughts from before with AI quite well and add new aspects.

EXTERNAL VS INTERNAL INFORMATION

The statement "External information dominates internal information" can be interpreted in several ways, so here are a few possible answers:

1. In terms of decision-making: This statement suggests that people
rely more heavily on external information (such as news, social media,
or opinions of others) when making decisions, rather than relying on
their internal thoughts, feelings, and intuition. While external
information can be useful, relying too much on it can lead to
conformity, groupthink, and a lack of creativity.

2. In terms of perception: This statement suggests that people's
perception of reality is more influenced by external
information than by
internal information. In other words, what we see and hear
from the
world around us shapes our understanding of what is real,
rather than
relying on our own internal experiences and beliefs.

3. In terms of learning: This statement suggests that people
learn more

from external sources (such as teachers, books, or the internet) than

from their own internal experiences. While external sources of
information can be valuable, it is important to also reflect on and learn

from one's own experiences.

In general, it is difficult to say whether external information dominates internal information, as both types of information are important and necessary for different aspects of human cognition and behavior. Ultimately, it depends on the context and the individual.

AI will continue to increase the proportion of external information

It is likely that AI will continue to increase the proportion of external information that people have access to and rely on. AI systems are designed to collect, process, and analyze vast amounts of data from a variety of sources, and they can provide insights and recommendations that may not be available to humans otherwise.

For example, AI-powered search engines and recommendation systems can help people discover new information and products, while AI-powered personal assistants and chatbots can provide personalized advice and support. Additionally, AI-powered decision-making tools can help businesses and governments make more informed decisions based on data analysis and predictive modeling.

While AI can be a powerful tool improving decision-making and increasing access to information, there are also potential risks and concerns. For example, AI algorithms may be biased or have unintended consequences, and there are concerns about privacy and security as more personal data is collected and analyzed by AI systems.

Therefore, it is important to approach the use of AI in a thoughtful and responsible way, with appropriate safeguards and regulations in place to ensure that the benefits of AI are maximized while minimizing the risks.

What role does internal and external information play in new thinking with AI?

Internal and external information play important roles in new thinking with AI.

Internal information, such as personal experiences, beliefs, and values, can provide valuable insights and perspectives that can help shape the development and application of AI systems. For example, AI developers may draw on their own experiences and insights to create AI systems that are more intuitive and user-friendly, or to design algorithms that are more inclusive and unbiased.

External information, on the other hand, is critical for training and testing AI systems. AI systems are only as good as the data they are trained on, and the quality and diversity of that data is essential for ensuring that AI systems are accurate and reliable. Additionally, external information can provide valuable context and feedback that can help refine and improve AI systems over time.

However, it is important to recognize that both internal and external information can be subject to bias and other limitations. Therefore, it is important to approach the use of AI in a thoughtful and responsible way, with appropriate safeguards and regulations in place to ensure that the benefits of AI are maximized while minimizing the risks. This may include strategies such a transparent and inclusive data collection, ongoing monitoring and evaluation of AI system, and stakeholder engagement to ensure that diverse perspectives are represented in the development and application of AI.

It is something completely different whether we ourselves mov in a landscape and take in information through our senses, or let a landscape pass by on the screen, which is commented on by a speaker. In addition to reality, TV and YouTube Videos, the metaverse is now also appearing on the horizon, promising to offer us further extraneous information. Consequently, we have to be careful not to completely lose the balance between our own and external information. This could well be a scenario that we have to reckon with due to AI.

My point is not to continually bring nostalgia into the consideration, but it does seem remarkable to me that decades ago I wrote the following: What external information is, is pretty clear. All information that is transmitted by media. Own information on the other hand can originate only locally. One must have been there oneself. However, they can also arise in the head itself – then they are ideas.

OPPORTUNITIES OF TODAY'S YOUTH WITH AI

Although it cannot necessarily be assumed that I was once a youth myself, because that was a very long time ago, fortunately there is proof that I made written contributions on the subject back in the 1980s. For example, I wrote this text at the time, and I have no intention of retracting a single word of it:

"Young people have a fine sense for wrong tones. Actually, it's not new at all when people talk about new morals, new sensitivity, new tenderness. I think there is a very broad, very deep movement among young people toward an uncompromising sincerity. This turn to plain speaking is also a result of better articulation skills.

Today's adults have grown up in a world characterized by deprivation and effort. At least in their majority. In this world, there was no room for hedonism, excessive sensibility and alternatives. There was only one direction in the two decades after World War II: forward, in doubt with elbows rather than without. No one reflected in a big way, no one looked back.

Today's young people have almost all grown up in affluence. The distance to having and wanting has become very small. In addition, a number of reality brakes have been added; today, young people simply know more. They know the overall economic situation, they know the situation on the housing market and with jobs, with pension insurance, with finite raw materials. Facts had led to reflection.

Knowing this, consideration of whether the parent's thinking makes sense at all is almost inevitable. Basically, it is not at all difficult for many young people to answer this question partially in the negative. Many young people therefore reject performance neuroses and dream of the California Life Style. Not always suspecting that this goes hand in hand with considerable intellectual achievements. A conspicuously deep information gap! In Silicon Valley, techno-narcissism is taken to the extreme and takes on almost drug-like forms with so-called happy technology."

Of course, one could the position that what is over 40 years old is no longer of interest to anyone. But that's not true at all, because we are facing a whole new challenge with the AI revolution. Engaging with history in this context can be illuminating for new thinking.

It is somewhat surprising that without the rich entrepreneur Friedrich Engels (1820 – 1895) Karl Marx's "Capital" would never been written. Engels, much like many young people today, noticed at the time that his father's charity work did not cure poverty. Engels studied the discrepancy between capital and labor in England – and not only there, where it was worst. He was sensitive enough to recognize that something could be fundamentally wrong here. Just as many young people today recognize that democracy may be the best form of government, but new norms and values need to be worked out.

Typical for the young people in our time is in many countries: They are intelligent, know relatively much – but it is difficult for them to convert their knowledge and abilities into an activity corresponding to them. In an activity that they like and that is recognized by society. Added to this are climate change, pandemics, inflation and wars. What role can AI play in improving the overall situation?

How can I find a functional work-life balance?

Achieving a functional work-life balance can be challenging, but there are several strategies that you can use to help you to find a balance that works for you. Here are some tips that may help:

1. Set clear boundaries: Establish clear boundaries between your work
and personal life. For example, set specific work hours and stick to
them, and avoid checking your work email or taking work calls outside
of those hours.

2. Prioritize self-care: Make sure to prioritize self-care activities such as
exercise, healthy eating, and getting enough sleep. These activities can
help you maintain your energy and focus, and reduce stress levels.

3. Be realistic about workload: Don't take on more work than you can
handle. Be honest with yourself and your employer about availability
and capacity.

4. Lean to delegate: If possible, delegate tasks that can be done by
others. This can help reduce your workload and free up time for other
activities.

5. Take breaks: Take regular breaks throughout the day, even if they are
short. This can help you recharge and refocus.

6. Communicate with your employer: If you're struggling to maintain
a work-life balance, talk to your employer about possible

solutions.

They may be able to offer more flexible working arrangements or

support.

Remember that finding a functional work-life balance is a personal process, and what works for one person may not work for another. Be patient in finding the balance that work best for you.

Can AI help me to find a suitable job?

Yes, AI can help me to find a suitable job in several ways. Here are some examples:

1. Job search platforms: AI-powered job search platforms like LinkedIn

and Indeed use machine learning algorithms to match your skills and

experience with relevant job openings. They can help you find job

opportunities that match your criteria and preferences.

2. Resume screening: Many companies use AI-powered tools to screen

resumes and cover letters. These tools can quickly scan through a large

number of applications and identify the most qualified candidates based

on their skills and experience.

3. Interview preparation: AI-powered interview preparation tools like

Mya and InterviewBit can help you prepare for job interviews by

providing feedback on your answers and identifying areas where you

need to improve.

4. Career development: AI-powered career development platforms like

Eightfold and Gloat use machine learning algorithms to analyze your

skills and experience and suggest career paths and development

opportunities that match your interests and strengths.

While AI can be a helpful tool in your job search, it's important to remember that it's just one part of the process. It's still important to network, customize your application, and prepare for interviews on your own.

What do I have to consider in order to network successfully?

Networking can be a powerful tool in building your career, but it's important to approach it in the right way to be successful. Here are some things to consider:

1. Set clear goals: Before attending such an event or reaching out to

someone, make sure you have a clear goal in mind. What do you hope

to gain from this connection? Are you looking for job opportunities,

mentorship, or industry insights?

2. Do your research: Research the people or organizations you want to

network with and learn as much as you can about them. This will help

you make a stronger connection and demonstrate your interest and

knowledge.

3. Be authentic: Networking is about building relationships, so be

genuine and authentic in your interactions. Don't try to be

someone
you're not or oversell yourself.

4. Be respectful of people's time: When reaching out to someone, be
respectful of their time and availability. Be clear and concise in your
communication and don't be pushy or demanding.

5. Follow up: After meeting someone, be sure to follow up with a thank-
you note or email. This shows that you appreciate their time and are
interested in staying in touch.

6. Give back: Networking is a two-way street, so be sure to offer
something of value to the people you connect with. This could be
sharing your own expertise or offering to help in some way.

Remember that networking is a long-term process, and building a relationship takes time and effort. Be patient and persistent, and don't be discouraged if you don't see immediate results.

With all these points listed, even more can be worked into the details with the help of AI. Effective networking is very important to a career today. Not only as an employee, but also if you become self-employed at some point. As an author, I was a partner in four companies at the same time and advised several others. It was a functioning network back then, even if we didn't call it that. Today with AI, there is certainly a much bigger wheel that can be turned if you take the right steps.

What is an authentic person?

An authentic person is someone who is genuine, honest, and true to themselves in their words and actions. Authenticity is about being true to your own values, beliefs, and personality, rather than performing to what others expect of you.

Some traits of an authentic person include:

1. Self-awareness: An authentic person has a good understanding of
   their own strengths, weaknesses, and emotions. They are honest with
   themselves about their own flaws and imperfections.

2. Honesty: An authentic person is truthful and transparent in their
   communication. They don't hide behind lies or try to manipulate others
   for personal gain.

3. Consistency: An authentic person is consistent in their behavior and
   actions. They don't change their values or beliefs to fit in with different
   groups or situations.

4. Empathy: An authentic person has empathy and understanding for
   others. They are able to connect with others on a deep level and show
   genuine care and concern.

5. Self-acceptance: An authentic person accepts themselves for who
   they are, including their strengths and weaknesses. They don't try to
   be someone they're not or pretend to have qualities they don't possess.

Being authentic is not always easy, as it requires courage and vulnerability. However, it can lead to greater self-awareness, stronger relationships, and a more fulfilling life.

STRATEGY THEORY

We should make one thing very clear to ourselves from the outset: Strategies are objectives and goals are points, not scales. Imagine a target, where the meeting point in the middle is the most important point. It's just one point and it's not two or three! The reason I mention this is because a lot of strategies aren't to the point, that's the biggest mistake! If you are wondering, why you need strategies at all: If you want to become an authentic personality and be successful in your job, you have to be able to solve complex problems and tasks. This also applies to your private life, because here, too, decisions have to be made that decisively
determine the life of your family and your own.

Now, in the age of artificial intelligence (AI), it is particularly important that you have a basic knowledge of strategic theory so that you can ask the right questions straight to the point on most topics.

What is Strategy Theory?

At its core, strategy theory aims to provide insights into how organizations can make decisions in the face of uncertainty and complexity. It draws on a range of disciplines, including economics, psychology, sociology, and organizational behavior, to develop frameworks and models that can help organizations to formulate and execute effective strategies.

Which strategies make sense for people?

Just like organizations, individuals can benefit from developing and execution effective strategies to achieve their personal goals and objectives. Here are some strategies that can make sense for people:

1. Goal Setting: Define clear and specific goals is an essential first step

in developing a personal strategy. Goals can help individuals to focus

their efforts and prioritize their time and resources.

2. Time Management: Effective time management is critical to achieving

personal goals. Strategies such as prioritization, delegation, and

scheduling can help individuals to make the most of their time and

avoid distraction.

3. Skill Development: Developing new skills and competencies can help

individuals to achieve their personal and professional goals. Continuous

learning and skill-building can improve an individual's marketability and

increase their earning potential.

4. Networking: Building a strong network of professional and personal

contacts can be a valuable strategy for achieving personal goals.

Networking can provide access to new opportunities, information, and

support.

5. Financial Planning: Developing a sound financial plan can help

individuals to achieve their financial goals and build wealth over time.

Strategies such as budgeting, saving, and investing can help individuals
to manage their finances effectively.

6. Health and Wellness: Prioritizing health and wellness can help
individuals to achieve their personal goals and lead a more fulfilling life.
Strategies such as exercise, health eating, and stress management can
help individuals to maintain physical and mental well-being.

It is extremely important that we not only understand which strategies are suitable for us in which fields, but also that we get to the theoretical core of strategy formulation. Anyone who pulls himself together to formulate a strategy must ask the question: What do I want to achieve? Answering this question can never be easy, because it unmistakably calls for analytic thinking! The danger is that thoughts or discussions often lead to proposed solutions instead of stating the goal. Of course, if the goal isn't clear, it's easy to come up with solutions that more or less miss the mark. However, it is about hitting the target very precisely so that the measure works as well as possible.

With the help of AI, it is now possible to narrow down the target than was sometimes possible in the past. This can be a valuable achievement, especially when in comes to the main promise to your customers or the main benefit to yourself.

Main promise or main benefit

Thesis: There is no strategy without main benefit for the one who uses it.

The problem is: there can be several main benefits of almost equal rank and then the problem is to determine the ranking. Because strategies are stronger when they focus on one benefit. Multiple claims cannot be strategically unique! Strategies are fundamentally unsuited to incorporate everything that is known. For they are working papers that must not be understood only by those who formulated them.

Thesis: The definition of the target group tends to be too broad.

Target groups can include one person (you!) or millions of people. If the strategy is personal and only concerns you, it is important you only need to make sure that it addresses your exact needs. But as soon as the communication involves media, the content affects a different number of people. Individuals can be targeted via the internet, and this personalized approach will be fare more precisely controlled by AI as today.

Thesis: Benefits need a credible justification or strong emotions!

A common info gap in personal life as well as in business is not looking for unique distinguishing features, but straight away for an ideology. I think this approach is remarkably short-sighted, even though I know that emotions can influence our decisions. If I can choose, I'd like to know the facts, assuming there are any.

Whenever a strategy is to be formulated as simply as possible, which is the indispensable prerequisite for its quality and effectiveness, the process becomes particularly difficult. Concentrating on the essentials in strategic work and at the same time on the new is a thinking process that moves in narrow leeway in the final phase. Truth and clarity are particularly important in this area, because every word is directly related to conceptual consequences. AI can accompany and further improve this process in the future.

Should opinions be true and logical?

The truth is a statement that can be supported to be true or false by data or evidence. In contrast, an opinion is a personal expression of a person's
feelings or thoughts that may or may not be based in data.

Many of our opinions are based on emotions, personal history, and values – all of which can be completely unsupported by meaningful evidence. Everyone is entitled to their opinion. But not all opinions are equally valuable. Opinions based in fact are more valuable than those that are not.

Thesis: Opinions always belong to individuals, facts to everyone!

That's not to say that everyone knows the facts and those who have an opinion sometimes don't believe it isn't based on fact. People are confident in their opinions and already think that their opinion is true and of course reflects the evidence. Why worry about the fact/opinion distinction? One very important reason is that precise thinking depends on our opinions and the facts available to us. AI allows us to make our opinions more thoughtful and informed.

What does the fact/opinion distinction do for us?

The fact/opinion distinction is an important tool that helps us differentiate between statements that are based on objective evidence and statements that are based on personal beliefs, values and preferences.

Facts are statements that can be objectively verified through empirical evidence, observations, or measurements. They are independent of personal biases, opinions, or beliefs. For example, "the earth is round" is a fact that can be supported by scientific evidence.

Opinions, on the other hand, are statements that express personal beliefs, preferences, or values. They are based on personal interpretations, experiences, or emotions. For example, "pizza is the best food" is an opinion that is subjective and cannot be verified through empirical evidence.

The fact/opinion distinction is important because it helps us to critically evaluate information and arguments. It enables us to distinguish between reliable information that is based on evidence and unsupported claims that are based on personal bias or opinion.

In everyday life, the fact/opinion distinction helps us make informed decisions about important issues. For example, when we are presented with conflicting information about a political candidate or a health treatment, we can use our understanding of the fact/opinion distinction to evaluate the credibility of the sources and the evidence they present.

Overall, the fact/opinion distinction is a valuable tool for critical thinking and effective communication. It enables us to navigate complex issues and make informed decisions based on reliable information.

What role does AI play in this sector?

AI plays a significant role in the fact/opinion distinction sector by assisting in the identification and classification of statements as either fact or opinion.

One application of AI in this sector is through natural language processing (NLP) techniques. NLP algorithms can analyze text data and identify patterns, relationships, and meanings in language use. By analyzing linguistic features such as sentence structure, vocabulary, and context, NLP algorithms can classify statements as either fact or opinion.

Another application of AI in this sector is through machine learning algorithms. These algorithms can be trained on large datasets of labeled text data to recognize patterns and make predictions about new data. For example, a machine learning model can be trained on a dataset of new articles labeled as either fact or opinion, and then used to classify new articles as either fact or opinion based on the patterns it has learned.

AI can also assist in fact-checking by automatically comparing statements to a database of known facts and verifying their accuracy. Fact-checking algorithms can be trained on large datasets of verified facts and can use NLP techniques to analyze statements and match them against relevant facts.

Overall, AI has the potential to improve the accuracy and efficiency of the fact/opinion distinction sector by automating the identification and classification of statements, as well as assisting in fact-checking and verification. However, it is important to note that AI is not infallible and must be carefully monitored and validated to ensure accuracy and fairness.

WHICH TOPICS ARE READERS MOST INTERESTED IN RELATED TO AI?

Based on my interactions with users and analysis of search trends, some of the topics related to AI that readers are most interested in include:

1. **Machine learning:** This is one of the most popular and widely discussed topics in the field of AI. Readers are interested in

learning
about the different types of machine learning algorithms,

their
applications, and how they can be used
to solve real-world problems.

2. **Natural Language Processing (NLP):** NLP is an area of AI that focuses on enabling machines to understand and interpret

human

language. Readers are interested in learning about the latest developments in NLP, including how it is being used to

improve search
engines, chatbots, and virtual assistants.

3. Computer Vision: Computer vision is a subfield of AI that

focuses on
enabling machines to interpret and understand visual

information.

Readers are interested in learning about the latest advances in
computer vision, including how it is being used in

autonomous vehicles,
surveillance systems, and facial recognition technology.

4. Robotics: Robotics is an area of AI that focuses on developing
intelligent machines that can perform tasks autonomously.

Readers are
interested in learning about the latest advances in robotics,

including
how robots are being used in manufacturing, healthcare, and

other
industries.

5. Ethics and Bias in AI: As AI becomes more pervasive, readers

are
interested in understanding the ethical implications of its use,

as well as
the potential for bias in AI systems. Topics related to AI ethics

and

bias, including private concerns, algorithms fairness, and

transparency,

are increasingly important to readers.

Basic Knowledge about Machine Learning

Machine Learning is a subfield of Artificial Intelligence (AI) that focuses on developing algorithms and statistical models that enable computer systems to learn from data and make predictions or decisions without being explicitly programmed.

Here are some concepts related to Machine Learning:

1. Supervised Learning: This type of learning involves training a model

with labeled data, where the input data is accompanied by a correct output or label. The model then uses this labeled data to make predictions on the new data.

2. Unsupervised Learning: This type of learning involves training a

model with unlabeled data, where the model must identify patterns or

relationships in the data on its own.

3. Reinforcement Learning: This type of learning involves training a

model to make decisions based on rewards or punishments. The model

learns by interacting with an environment and receiving feedback in the

form of rewards or punishments for its actions.

4. Data Preprocessing: This involves cleaning and transforming raw data into a format that can be used by machine learning algorithms.

This includes tasks such as removing missing values, scaling features,

and encoding categorical variables.

5. Model Training: This involves using an algorithm to build a model by

adjusting its parameters to fit the training data. This is done by

minimizing a cost function that measures the differences between the

model's predictions and the actual labels.

6. Model Evaluation: This involves assessing the performance of a

trained model on a new data that was not used in the training process.

Common evaluation metrics include accuracy, precision, recall, and F1

score.

7. Overfitting and Underfitting: Overfitting occurs when a model is too

complex and fits the training data too closely, leading to poor

performance on new data. Underfitting occurs when a model is too

simple and does not capture the underlying patterns in the data, also

leading to poor performance.

Machine learning algorithms are used in a wide range of applications, including image and speech recognition, natural language processing, fraud detection, recommendation systems, and predictive maintenance, among others.

Basic Knowledge about NLP

Natural Language Processing (NLP) is a subfield of artificial intelligence (AI) and computational linguistics that focuses on enabling computers to understand, interpret, and generate human language. Here are some basic concepts related to NLP:

1. Tokenization: This involves breaking down a piece of text into smaller
 units called tokens, such as words or subwords, to facilitate further
 processing.

2. Part-of-Speech (POS) Tagging: This involves assigning a part of
 speech to each word in a text, such as noun, verb, or adjective, to
 enable deeper analysis of the text.

3. Named Entity Recognition (NER): This involves identifying and
 extraction named entities from a text, such as people, organizations,
 and locations.

4. Sentiment Analysis: This involves determining the sentiment or
 emotion expressed in a piece of text, such as positive, negative, or
 neutral.

5. Language Modeling: This involves building statistical models that can
 predict the probability of a sequence of words or sentences occurring in
 a language.

6. Machine Translation: This involves translating text from one
 language to another using machine learning algorithms.

7. Text Summarization: This involves generating a shorter summary of

a longer piece of text while retaining its most important information.

NLP is used in a wide range of applications, such as chatbots, virtual assistants, sentiment analysis in social media, machine translation, text classification, information extraction, and speech recognition, among others.

Basic Knowledge about Computer Vision

Computer vison is a field of study focused on enabling machines to interpret and understand the visual world, which includes images and videos. Here are some basic concepts related to computer vision:

1. **Image processing:** It involves modifying or enhancing an image to
    improve its quality, extract useful information or remove unwanted
    information.

2. **Object detection:** It involves detecting the presence and location of
    objects within an image or video.

3. **Image segmentation:** It involves dividing an image into different
    regions or segments based on their characteristics, such as color,
    texture or brightness.

4. **Feature extraction:** It involves identifying key features in an image,
    such as edges, corners or textures, which can be used to recognize
    objects.

5. **Machine learning:** It is used to train models to recognize

objects or
perform other tasks in computer vision. Common machine learning
algorithms include deep learning, neural networks and decision tree.

6. Deep learning: It is a subset of machine learning that uses artificial
neural networks to recognize pattern in data.

7. Convolutional neural networks (CNNs): They are a type of deep
neural network designed to analyze images and videos by processing
them in small, overlapping squares called "convolutional kernels".

8. Optical character recognition (OCR): It involves recognizing text
within the image or video and converting it into machine-readable
format.

9. Facial recognition: It involves identifying and verifying a person's
identity based on their facial features.

10. Object tracking: It involves following an object's motion over time
within a video.

Basic Knowledge about Robotics

Robotics is a multidisciplinary field that involves the design, construction, operation, and use of robots. A robot is a machine that is programmed to carry out a set of tasks automatically, usually with some degree of autonomy.

Some basic knowledge about robotics includes:

1. Robot Components: A robot consists of three main components: the
   mechanical structure, the sensors and actuators, and the control
   system.

2. Types of Robots: Robots can be classified into different types based
   on their design, mobility, and application. Some common types include
   industrial robots, mobile robots, humanoid robots, and medical robots.

3. Robot Programming: Robot Programming involves creating the
   software that controls the robot's actions. This can be done using
   programming languages such as C++, Python, or MATLAB.

4. Robot Sensors: Sensors are essential components of a robot, as they
   allow the robot to perceive and interact with its environment. Common
   sensors used in robotics include cameras, LIDAR, sonar, and tactile
   sensors.

5. Robot Actuators: Actuators are the components that enable the robot
   to move and perform actions. These include motors, servos, and
   pneumatic or hydraulic systems.

6. Robot Control System: The control system is responsible for
   coordinating the robot's actions and ensuring that it performs its tasks
   correctly. This can involve feedback control, motion planning,

and
   obstacle avoidance.

7. Robot Applications: Robotics has a wide range of applications, from
   manufacturing and assembly to healthcare, exploration, and
   entertainment.

8. Robots Ethics: As robots become more advanced and ubiquitous,
   there are ethical considerations that need to be addressed, such as
   safety, privacy, and impact on employment.

Overall, robotics is an exciting and rapidly evolving field that has the potential to transform many areas of our lives. By the way, I saw my first pair of robots in Berlin in 1963. All they could do was avoid each other. A few things have changed since then!

Basic Knowledge about Ethics and Bias in AI

Ethics and bias in AI are two critical topics in the development and deployment of artificial intelligence systems. Here are some basic concepts to understand:

1. Ethics in AI: Ethic in AI refers to the moral principles that should
   guide the development and use of AI systems. This includes issues such
   as accountability, transparency, privacy, and fairness. Ethical
   considerations in AI also encompass questions about the social impact
   of these technologies and the implications for human values and rights.

2. Bias in AI: Bias in AI refers to the systematic error or inaccuracies that
   can occur in AI systems due to human bias or data bias. This

can lead
to unfair or discriminatory outcomes in areas such as employment,
healthcare, and criminal justice.

3. Types of Bias: There are various types of bias that can occur in AI
systems, including sampling bias, algorithmic bias, and user bias. For
example, algorithmic bias can occur when AI systems are trained on
biased data, leading to discriminatory results.

4. Mitigating Bias: To mitigate bias in AI systems, developers can take
steps such as diversifying training data, performing regular audits and
testing, and developing fairness metrics to evaluate the performance of
the algorithms.

5. Explainability: Explainability refers to the ability to understand how
an AI system arrives at its decisions or predictions. This is an important
aspect of ethics in AI, as it can help ensure that these systems are
transparent and accountable.

6. Regulations and Standards: Governments and industry organizations
are developing regulations and standards to address ethics and bias in
AI. For example, the EU's General Data Protection Regulation (GDPR)
includes provisions on automated decision-making, while the IEEE has
developed a set of standards for ethical AI.

Overall, addressing ethics and bias in AI is essential for ensuring that these technologies are developed and deployed in a responsible and ethical manner that benefits society as a whole.

WHAT WILL AI BE ABLE TO DO IN THE FUTURE?

I think there will be a series of upheavals in various sectors over the next 10 years, the extend of which we cannot really imagine yet. That's why it's extremely important to be involved right from the start when it comes to applications.

MY FORMULA: NI + AI = IMPROVED HI

Our Natural Intelligence (NI) will always be different and subject to more or less fluctuations in individuals. But Artificial Intelligence (AI) will be relatively the same from the outset. Properly applied, this can dramatically increase human intelligence. To be precise, the intelligence of the individual hardly increases, but the performance can improve significantly.

How will AI transform the scientific method?

AI has the potential to significantly transform the scientific method by enhancing its capabilities, speeding up the pace of scientific discoveries, and providing new tools for analyzing and interpreting data. Here are some ways in which AI could transform the scientific method:

1. Data analysis: AI algorithms can analyze large datasets much faster
   and more accurately than humans, which can help researchers to
   identify patterns and correlations that might be missed using traditional
   methods.

2. Hypothesis generation: AI can generate hypotheses based on
   patterns in data, which can guide researchers towards new discoveries.

3. Experimentation: AI can help to design experiments by

identifying
the optimal conditions to test a hypothesis.

4. Prediction: AI models can predict the outcomes of experiments or the
behavior of complex systems, which can help researchers to refine their
hypotheses.

5. Automation: AI can automate many aspects of the scientific method,
from data collection to experiment design, which can reduce the time
and cost of research.

6. Collaboration: AI can facilitate collaboration between researchers by
providing a platform for sharing data, tools, and insights.

Overall, AI has the potential to transform the scientific method by enabling faster, mor accurate, and mor efficient scientific discoveries. However, it is important to note that AI is not a replacement of human intuition and creativity, and that it must be used in conjunction with traditional scientific methods to achieve the best results.

How will AI become a pillar of domestic and foreign policy?

AI has the potential to become a significant pillar of domestic and foreign policy in various ways. Here are some possible scenarios:

1. AI for domestic policy:

a. Policy formulation: AI can help in analyzing vast amounts of data to
identify patterns and trends that can inform policy formulation. For

example, AI can help in identifying areas of high crime rates, which can

inform policy decisions on how to allocate resources to curb crime.

b. Resource allocation: AI can help in optimizing resource allocation.

For example, AI can help in predicting the demand for healthcare

services, which can inform decision makers on resource allocation.

c. Monitoring and evaluation: AI can help in monitoring and evaluating

policy implementation. For example, AI can help in monitoring air

quality levels to ensure with environmental policies.

2. AI for foreign policy:

a. Geopolitical analysis: AI can help in analyzing geopolitical events and

trends. For example, AI can analyze news reports, social media posts,

and other sources of information to identify emerging trends and

potential threats.

b. Diplomacy: AI can help in diplomacy efforts by providing real-time

translation services, which can facilitate communication between

leaders who speak different languages.

c. International Trade: AI can help in identifying potential trading

partners and opportunities. For example, AI can help in identifying potential markets for products and services and predicting demand.

Overall, the integration of AI into domestic and foreign policy has the potential to provide policymakers with powerful tools for decision-making, resource allocation and diplomacy. However, it is crucial to ensure that these technologies are developed and deployed ethically and transparently to avoid unintended consequences.

How will AI enable next-gen consumer experiences?

AI has the potential to transform the way consumes experience products and services. Here are some ways AI can enable next-gen consumer experiences:

1. **Personalization:** AI can analyze customer data to personalize experience based on individual preferences and behavior. For example,
   recommending products, customizing interfaces, or providing targeted
   content.

2. **Predictive analytics:** AI can help predict consumer behavior and
   preferences, allowing companies to anticipate their needs and offer
   proactive solutions.

3. **Voice assistants:** AI-powered voice assistants like Siri and Alexa can
   help consumers interact with products and services in new ways,
   enabling hands-free and intuitive interactions.

4. **Augmented reality:** AI-powered AR can create immersive

experiences, allowing consumers to interact with products in new and
exciting ways. For example, trying on virtual clothes or testing out
furniture in a virtual space.

5. Chatbots: AI-powered chatbots can provide fast and efficient customer
service, answering questions and resolving issues 24/7.

6. Autonomous devices: AI-powered devices like drones and self-driving
cars can provide consumers with new levels of convenience and
accessibility.

Overall, AI has the potential to revolutionize the way companies engage with consumers, creating more personalized, convenient, and immersive experience.

How will AI want to overcome the climate crisis?

As an AI language model, I don't have wants or desires, but I can provide some insights on how AI can be used to help address the climate crisis.

AI can be used to help reduce greenhouse gas emissions by optimizing energy consumption and reducing waste. For example, machine learning algorithms can be used to predict energy usage and adjust building temperature and lighting accordingly to save energy. AI can also be used to optimize transportation routes, reducing fuel consumption and emissions.

AI can also be used to help mitigate the impact of climate change. For example, machine learning can be used to monitor and predict natural disasters, such as hurricanes and wildfires, allowing for more effective response and evacuation plans. AI can also be used to monitor and predict changes in ecosystems, such as changes in sea level or deforestation, allowing for proactive measures to be taken.

In addition, AI can be used to develop and improve renewable energy sources, such as wind and solar power, by analyzing data to optimize efficiency and reduce costs.

Overall, AI has the potential to play a significant role in addressing the climate crisis, by helping to reduce emissions, mitigate the impact of climate change, and develop sustainable energy sources. However, it's important to note that AI alone cannot solve the climate crisis, and a coordinated effort from governments, businesses, and individuals is needed to achieve significant progress in reducing greenhouse gas emissions and protect our planet.

How will AI enable truly personalized medicine?

AI has the potential to revolutionize personalized medicine by allowing for more precise and tailored treatments for individual patients. Here are some ways AI can enable personalized medicine:

1. **Analyzing patient data:** AI can analyze large amounts of patient
    data, including genomic data, medical history, and lifestyle factors, to
    identify patterns and correlations that can help diagnose and treat
    diseases more accurately. This can lead to more personalized treatment
    plans that take into account the unique characteristics of each patient.

2. **Predicting drug responses:** AI can be used to predict how patients
    will respond to certain drugs, based on their genomic and

clinical data.

This can help doctors choose the most effective treatment for each

patient, while minimizing side effects and adverse reactions.

3. Developing new drugs: AI can be used to analyze vast amounts of

data to identify new drug targets and potential drug compounds. This

can lead to the development of more targeted therapies that are

tailored to specific patient groups.

4. Real-time monitoring: AI can be used to monitor patient data in real-

time, allowing doctors to adjust treatment plans as needed based on

changes in the patient's condition. This can help ensure that patients

receive the most appropriate and effective treatment throughout the

course of their illness.

Overall, AI has the potential to transform personalized medicine by allowing for more precise and individualized treatments that take into account the unique characteristics of each patient. However, it's important to note that AI is not a replacement for human doctors and clinicians, but rather a tool that can support and enhance their expertise and decision-making.

Taken together, are AI and NI superior to previous human intelligence?

It's not accurate to compare AI and NI (Natural Intelligence) to previous human intelligence as they are fundamentally different.

AI refers to computer-based systems that can perform tasks that would typically require human intelligence, such as recognizing images, translating languages, and playing games. However, AI systems are limited to performing specific tasks and are only as good as the data they are trained on. They lack the broader cognitive abilities of human being, such as creativity, emotional intelligence, and commonsense reasoning.

On the other hand, human intelligence, or NI, is the ability of human beings to reason, solve problems, learn, and communicate using natural language. Human intelligence is flexible, adaptable, and creative, allowing us to perform a wide range of complex tsks that are beyond the capabilities of AI systems.

While AI has made significant advancements in recent years, it still lacks the cognitive abilities of human beings and is not capable of replicating human intelligence in its entirety. In some areas, AI may surpass human performance, such as recognizing patterns in large datasets of playing complex games, but in many other areas, human intelligence is still superior.

Therefore, AI and NI are not directly comparable or superior to each other, as they are different forms of intelligence with different strengths and limitations. Rather than viewing AI as a replacement for human intelligence, it's more productive to view AI as a toll that can augment human intelligence and help us solve complex problems more effectively.

What improvements can be expected in the near future?

There are several areas where we can expect significant improvements in the near future:

1. Natural Language Processing: Advances in natural language processing (NLP) technology are making it possible for computers to
understand and respond to human language more accurately then ever
before. This could lead to more sophisticated chatbots, voice

assistants,

and other applications that can interact with humans in a more natural

and intuitive way.

2. Computer Vision: Improvements in computer vision technology are

making it possible for computers to recognize and interpret images and

videos with greater accuracy. This could have significant applications in

fields such as healthcare, where AI could be used to analyze medical

images and diagnose diseases more accurately.

3. Robotics: Advances in robotics technology are making it possible for

robots to perform more complex tasks in a wide range of environments.

This could lead to more widespread adaption of robots in fields such as

manufacturing, logistics, and healthcare.

4. Autonomous Vehicles: Autonomous vehicle technology is rapidly

improving, with companies such as Tesla, Google, and Uber investing

heavily in the development of self-driving cars. This could lead to a

significant reduction in traffic accidents and fatalities, as well as

increased mobility for people who are unable to drive.

5. Healthcare: AI has the potential to revolutionize healthcare, with

applications ranging from personalized medicine to drug discovery to disease diagnosis. As AI technologies continue to improve, we can

expect to see more widespread adoption of AI in healthcare settings.

Overall, the future of AI looks bright, with continued advancements in technology expected to bring significant benefits to a wide range of industries and fields. However, it's important to note that there are also concerns around the impact of AI on jobs, privacy, and other social issues, which will need to be addressed as AI technology continues to evolve.

www.ingramcontent.com/pod-product-compliance
Lightning Source LLC
Chambersburg PA
CBHW071135220526
45467CB00015B/1020